How to Ma... 'L

Your Guide to ...ing a L......'d With Proven Processes and Systems to Maximise Your Rental Property Returns

Cal Shelton

www.calshelton.com

© Copyright 2020 - All rights reserved.

The content contained within this book may not be reproduced, duplicated or transmitted without direct written permission from the author or the publisher.

Under no circumstances will any blame or legal responsibility be held against the publisher, or author, for any damages, reparation, or monetary loss due to the information contained within this book, either directly or indirectly.

Legal Notice:

This book is copyright protected. It is only for personal use. You cannot amend, distribute, sell, use, quote or paraphrase any part, or the content within this book, without the consent of the author or publisher.

Disclaimer Notice:

Please note the information contained within this document is for educational and entertainment purposes only. All effort has been executed to present accurate, up to date, reliable, complete information. No warranties of any kind are declared or implied. Readers acknowledge that the author is not engaged in the rendering of legal, financial, medical or professional advice. The content within this book has been derived from various sources. Please consult a licensed professional before attempting any techniques outlined in this book.

By reading this document, the reader agrees that under no circumstances is the author responsible for any losses, direct or indirect, that are incurred as a result of the use of the information contained within this document, including, but not limited to, errors, omissions, or inaccuracies.

Table of Contents

Table of Contents

Introduction

Chapter 1: What Makes a Good Landlord?

   The Basic Responsibilities of a Landlord

   How to Be a Good Landlord

   Benefits of Being a Good Landlord

   Joining a Landlord's Association

Chapter 2: Getting Your Property Ready to Let

   Maintaining Your Property and Keeping Your Tenants Safe

   To Furnish or Not to Furnish?

   Checklist and Key Takeaways

Chapter 3: Marketing Your BTL

   What Do You Have to Offer?

   Reaching Your Audience

   Let's Talk About Rent

   Checklist and Key Takeaways

Chapter 4: Selecting Tenants

- Processing Applications
- Tenant Referencing
- Avoiding Bad Tenants
- Checklist and Key Takeaways

Chapter 5: Tenancy Agreements
- Agreements and Assured Shorthold Tenancy
- Guarantors
- Taking Inventory
- Taking a Deposit
- Documents to Give the Tenant
- Checklist and Key Takeaways

Chapter 6: Managing Your BTL
- Handing Over the Keys
- Maintaining the Property
- Collecting Rent
- Checklist and Key Takeaways

Chapter 7: Ending the Tenancy
- Lease Expiry
- Dealing with a Tenant Wanting to Leave Early
- Terminating a Lease Early

Updates to Section 8 and Section 21

Checklist and Key Takeaways

Chapter 8: Bookkeeping

Setting Up an Effective Bookkeeping System

Taxes

Checklist and Key Takeaways

Chapter 9: Should I Manage It Myself or Hire Someone?

Deciding on Using a Letting Agent

What Does a Letting Agent Do?

Property Management Software

Checklist and Key Takeaways

Conclusion

References

A gift to my readers

Included with your purchase of this book is the 9 Simple Checks to Make Before Any Tenant Moves In. In the 9 Simple Checks you will learn:

- What documents you must give your tenant before they move in
- The four steps you can take to make sure your rent is paid on time every month
- The resources I use to work through and check each item on the list

Click the link below and let me know the email address you would me to send it to.

www.calshelton.com

Introduction

Property is a great asset, especially if you have one that you are able to rent out. Many people buy properties and let them out, but do it by the seat of their pants and can end up running into many unexpected problems down the line. For instance, you may struggle to find tenants, your tenants may stop paying their rent, you might not be able to hold onto their deposit because you did not provide the "prescribed information", or maybe just not being able to hire the right property manager, or even decide if you need one. I'm sure you do not want to walk the path that feels like it is laden with BTL booby traps. That is why I'm going to provide you with the guidance and solutions you need to run your BTL successfully and do it with as few problems as possible.

This book will take a look at what it means to be a successful landlord. I will provide you with tips on how to deal with your tenants in the correct manner, retain the good ones, and avoid the bad ones. You will be introduced to concepts that you may not have even been aware of, like the various documents you need to present to the tenant or the importance of taking inventory. This

Introduction

book will give you the information you need to choose the right tenant, manage them well throughout their tenancy, and end a tenancy as smoothly as possible.

Managing your property portfolio is all about people management, effectively managing and communicating with your tenants. Otherwise, it will not be a good experience for you or your tenants. The tenants need to feel comfortable with having you as a landlord, which requires you to have confidence. This confidence can only come when you have a full understanding of the laws, regulations, and the general requirements of running a property. I want to help you navigate your legal requirements and point out key legislation you may not have known about. Once you are done with this book, you will be armed with the information you need to manage your property like a professional.

There are some common pitfalls and mistakes people make in the rental property space. Most of these mistakes are easily avoidable and are usually caused by a lack of preparation or knowledge. I will go through them and teach you how to avoid these situations. Whether it is understanding the responsibilities of a landlord or

Introduction

selecting the right property manager, the information is in this book.

I am a landlord myself and know the struggles of handling tenants, finances, and property upkeep all too well. I have also had the privilege of experiencing many successes through investing in property and creating a modest BTL portfolio, which provides me with a comfortable income. I do not claim to have the biggest portfolio, but I do offer my advice based on my own experience to those that are considering or are self-managing their own BTLs. I will share my experiences of being a landlord and will tell you the steps and systems I have used to make my life easier when managing my BTLs. Put simply, property is my obsession, and I enjoy every aspect of building and managing my property portfolio. In terms of being a landlord, historically, I have loved to be hands-on and have enjoyed getting involved in the management of my properties. However, more recently, I have been using property managers to free up more of my time to focus more on being an investor.

You, as the landlord, are ultimately liable for your BTL and your legal responsibilities as a landlord, not anyone else—not even your letting agent. This is why it is so important to have the right information available to you, know the necessary actions you need to take, and know what decisions need to be made. Being informed and aware will help you avoid fines, penalties, or even prison time. You want to be able to protect yourself from any unforeseen circumstances or situations.

Given today's view of landlords in the UK, it may be hard to believe that there is legislation available to protect the landlord as well as the tenants. If you are aware of your rights and that of your tenants, it will help you to navigate and resolve any issues you may face. You will also be able to handle your tenants in the right way, be able to resolve any disputes and foster a relationship of trust between you and your tenant. The bottom line is that this is your property, and you want to be able to take care of it and utilise it in the right way: the way that benefits you the most and gives you the most peace of mind.

As a landlord, you will be providing someone with a home, and you have the option of being as hands-on or hands-off as you like. Doing it right means higher returns for you from your property asset. The first step is having all the right information, and the next is to act on that knowledge. My hope is that you will gain all you need to

Introduction

run and successfully manage your BTLs, so you are free to live the life you have always wanted while also reaching your investing goals. With all that said, let's get started on your journey to becoming a successful landlord.

Chapter 1: What Makes a Good Landlord?

So you have decided to rent out your property and become a landlord. That is great! But it does require some knowledge beforehand. Because you are reading this book, you obviously want to be an effective and good landlord. Being a good landlord not only benefits the tenant but you as well through higher rents, reduced voids and greater peace of mind.

At the risk of stating the obvious, a landlord is someone who owns a property and is renting it out to other people for a sum of money. There are certain expectations and responsibilities that a landlord has, so it is not just renting out your property and stepping away from it. Understanding what your responsibilities are as a landlord will help you out along this journey.

Chapter 1: What Makes a Good Landlord?

The Basic Responsibilities of a Landlord

As a landlord, your overarching responsibility is to provide an adequate living space for your tenant. The property should be clean, safe, and overall just a good environment for the tenant to live. There should not be huge issues with the property. It needs to be a place where people would be satisfied to live.

Do a thorough check of the property and make sure it is a safe place to live. Remove any hazards and keep the property maintained well. If the tenant is unhappy with the living conditions or has discovered something potentially dangerous about the property, they might report you to the Council's Environment Health Department (NRLA, n.d.). This will not be good for you if the council deems serious repairs are needed to be a safe and healthy place for your tenants. This can result in council inspections and, in extreme cases, the council may take action against you to make good the property. Avoiding this is the better option, so just make sure you have checked your property thoroughly and that there is nothing that would put a tenants health at risk.

It is your responsibility to make sure that your insurance and mortgage providers are aware that you will be letting out your property. Be mindful of what is covered and what is allowed. You might also be able to get some insurance benefits, so make sure you chat with your insurance provider about this. They will also help you pick the best options, which will allow you to have the best coverage at the best price. Always do your research when it comes to things like this.

It is well within your rights to visit your property to make sure everything is going well and that the tenants are taking care of it. Just make sure you are courteous of your tenants. I'm sure you wouldn't want someone coming into your home unannounced. You must give a written notice of your visit, which should be presented to your tenants at least 24 hours before you plan on visiting. The notice can be sent by email, as long as you ask them to reply so that you know they have agreed. If they do not agree to the visit because it is not a suitable time or for any other valid reason, you should cancel and reschedule it for another time. The more notice you give the tenant,

Chapter 1: What Makes a Good Landlord?

the better. This way, you avoid any scheduling conflicts. It is important to have a good relationship with your tenants, as it will make these sorts of situations much easier.

Repairs are also a landlord's responsibility, especially when it comes to big things like burst pipes, mould, wiring, and the general structure of the building. This will all fall on you, so make sure that the property is well taken care of before renting it out. Of course, smaller things, like changing light bulbs and unclogging drains, will fall on the tenants. The tenants also have a responsibility to take care of the items in the home, so if they break anything, it will be their responsibility to fix it. Make sure the contract explicitly states that.

As a landlord, it is your job to remove any confusion or misunderstandings that may happen. Make sure that the tenant clearly understands their responsibilities, and make sure that the lease covers both you and them. You should never proceed with anything unless you have the right paperwork. Rent, payment structure, and when the rent needs to be paid must be clearly indicated in the lease. These things are just a quick overview of what a landlord needs to be aware of. I will go more into detail about specifics as the book progresses.

How to Be a Good Landlord

There is a lot of negative stigma around landlords and plenty of news stories of people speaking about how awful their experiences have been renting. A quick google of "landlord fine" will bring up plenty of news articles of unethical and illegal practices. We do not want to be this type of landlord. Having a good relationship with your tenant and providing them with great service is the foundation of being a good landlord. There are a few things you can do to make the experience pleasant for your tenants, to build a good relationship, and to foster trust.

Communication

Almost all problems can be overcome through effective communication with your tenant. Communication builds trust, and it makes sure that both parties are on the same

Chapter 1: What Makes a Good Landlord?

page. This has to be the basis of the tenant and landlord relationship, and it must be fostered at the beginning.

The first step to good communication is being present and approachable. Your tenants should feel as though they can come to you with questions or problems. When they first move in, show up and welcome them to their new home. If you want to go the extra mile, bring them over a welcome gift or write them a welcome letter. This will already make them feel welcome and as if they can trust you.

Make sure you are dressed appropriately. You want to look professional since property management is a business and should be treated as one. If you treat it as a business and your tenants as customers, you will act more professionally and take care of your tenants well. Of course, you don't have to rent out a tuxedo every time you see them or visit the house, but try not to go there in a tracksuit. It is a small thing, but it increases your credibility.

Doing simple things like showing them around the house when they first move in will do wonders for your relationship. Show them which tap is for hot water and which is for cold. Guide them to anything they might

Chapter 1: What Makes a Good Landlord?

need to know and allow them to ask questions. If they have any questions or concerns at that point, answer them in a friendly manner.

Make sure that you and your tenant have gone over the agreement and that they understand what is required of them, as well as understanding what you are providing. This will help limit any uncomfortable conversations down the line. Whatever can be aired out and resolved before they move in, or at the beginning of the tenancy, will result in a much smoother ride in the future.

Your tenants should have your number and email address, should they need to contact you. If something goes wrong or if they need to get a hold of you for any reason, you should be available to them. You can give all of this information in a welcome note. Of course, you don't want to be bothered in the middle of the night with minor issues. To prevent this from happening, you can state the times in which you would be available to take calls or read emails. If you are going away or are just not going to be available for a few days or weeks, make sure that your tenants are aware of this and that you provide them with the contact details of someone who would be able to help them with something, should the need arise.

Chapter 1: What Makes a Good Landlord?

Creating boundaries and putting steps in place like this will increase the ease of communication on both your parts.

Be Responsive to Your Tenants

Now that you have made your tenants feel welcome and have created an open line of communication between you, you must follow through. Your tenants will contact you if there are any problems or if they have requests, so be available to listen to them. Yes, there may be some requests that seem silly to you, but do your best to see what you can do. At the end of the day, your tenants are your customers.

If it is in your power to fix the problem immediately, do so. There is nothing more frustrating for a tenant than having to wait an extremely long time for a small problem to be resolved. If it is a large job, then explain to the tenant that it might take a bit longer to fix the problem. This goes back to communication. It is better to be honest with them from the beginning so that they are aware of what is going on.

Chapter 1: What Makes a Good Landlord?

In the case of big problems and things that need to be repaired more immediately, it is a good idea to have relationships with tradesmen that can help. Building these relationships and having the contacts beforehand will result in you being able to make the repairs at a much quicker rate. Never just do things for the sake of doing things; make sure that the job will be done well. This is still your property, so take care of it as if you were living in it. Having repairs done badly and quickly will end up costing you more in the long run. If you haven't worked with any tradesmen or don't have any that come recommended to you, there are online resources such as checkatrade.com where you can find qualified people that have received reviews from previous jobs. You can post a job, receive quotes and assess each applicant for the work.

Your tenants may also have other requests that they think will make the property better overall. It would be a good idea to listen to these requests. If you have to rent out the property again, most of the issues would have been ironed out. That will relieve pressure off you down the line, and any future tenants will have fewer complaints.

Chapter 1: What Makes a Good Landlord?

Give Your Tenants Space

As much as you should be available for your tenants, you shouldn't be a helicopter mom to your property. If you are constantly getting in contact with your tenants or always wanting to pop in for a visit, they will get fed up. You should respect their privacy and allow them to enjoy their home.

You are entitled to do inspections and visit the property, but besides this you should allow your tenants their freedom. You also do not need to do inspections every week or every month, and if you are planning on visiting, make sure you have informed them in advance. Tenants won't be happy if they constantly have to prepare for a visit from their landlord. Even friendly visits are not appropriate. You shouldn't try to be their friend. Allow them to have their space, and they will respect you a lot more.

Chapter 1: What Makes a Good Landlord?

Keep Up to Date with the Legal Requirements

Being a good landlord isn't all about getting along with your tenants. That is a very small piece of the whole puzzle. As the landlord, it is your responsibility to be up to date with all the legal requirements that you need to fulfil. Legal requirements regarding tenancies are continually changing and being updated, but it isn't a good enough excuse to say you didn't know.

The best thing you can do is to keep yourself up to date by continually researching, or even taking courses. There are multiple landlord courses out there, and the curriculum will always be updated to the current laws and what is going on in the property market at that moment. Register with a landlord association and complete their property management course to become fully informed of all your requirements and of best practices (some associations are listed at the end of this chapter). If you have a holistic knowledge of the property market, you will also be able to advise or help your tenants if need be.

Chapter 1: What Makes a Good Landlord?

Benefits of Being a Good Landlord

When you are a good landlord who takes care of their property and their tenants, you will reap the benefits. These benefits are not just immediate but will run into the future. Everything you do now to better the property and make the current tenants happy will provide dividends in the future. Then, you will be pleased that you made the extra effort.

Retain Tenants

Good tenants can be hard to find, so if you are lucky enough to have them, you should aim to keep them for as long as possible. You want to retain your tenants for long periods of time as it will result in a lot less work for you. Trying to get new tenants can cost more money, and there is no guarantee that you will find someone immediately.

If a tenant moves out because they are unhappy, it can bring your reputation down. You would be surprised how far negative comments can travel, and that could hurt your business. You should always be doing your best so that people have good things to say about your letting business so that they want to stay or may refer a friend when they decide to move out.

Many landlords do their best not to have any void periods. A void is any time your property does not have a tenant. Your mortgage still has to be paid, which will now fall on you. The best way to avoid this is to have long-standing tenants. Happy tenants will want to stay, and that creates less work for you. Plus, if you keep your tenants, you will always know what to expect, and you will have spent the necessary time getting to know them. This will mean fewer problems popping up and fewer issues for you to deal with overall. You can rest easy knowing that you will be getting consistent rent and that there is less risk for you.

Easier to Get New Tenants

Part of being a good landlord is taking care of your property. If your property is well taken care of, the house will be easier to rent out again if the current tenants move out. Sometimes, there is nothing you can do to prevent someone from moving out. If they are moving cities, downsizing, or upgrading, then it is out of your control. Making sure that your tenants enjoyed their stay and that the property was well looked after will be beneficial when looking for new tenants. Just as negative comments can spread, positive ones can also. Plus, perhaps your old tenants will be able to refer to new ones. This may not happen very often, but honestly, you never know.

If a tenant leaves and you have a lot of work to do in the house before you can rent it out again, this can seriously harm your income. You will need to first sort out any issues and fix up the house before you can attract new tenants. If this were all done while the old tenants were living in the house, it would cut down on the time the property is left vacant. The quicker you can get new tenants, the better for you.

Confidence That You Aren't Breaking Any Laws

There are plenty of laws that govern the property market. Being a good landlord means that you are aware of these laws, and you're sure you are following them. The laws are there to protect both you and the tenant, although it can feel as though the tenant benefits more. Regardless of whether we like the laws or not, we have to follow them.

Making sure you are adhering to the laws and regulations will give you security in the fact that no one can turn around and accuse you of not doing something the right way. When it comes to property, because it is someone's home, things can escalate quickly. You may need to defend your actions in court someday. If you have all your ducks in a row, you will have a solid defence even if a case does get escalated to court. This is especially true if you end up in the unfortunate situation of having to evict a tenant through the courts.

More Stable Income and Higher Returns

If you are a horrible landlord, chances are people are not going to want to stay. This will affect the amount of money you have coming in. The higher the turnover of tenants, the more likely you are of having periods where your property will not bring in money. No landlord wants that, so if you do manage to find good tenants, you should be doing what you can to keep them. If you want your

Chapter 1: What Makes a Good Landlord?

income to be stable, then it does pay to be a competent landlord.

Joining a Landlord's Association

A landlord's association is a space where you can get help and support in the rental sector. They can give you advice on specific problems and keep you up to date with the laws and regulations. Laws are continuously changing, so it is good to keep up to date with what is going on.

Each landlord association may vary slightly in what they provide, but in general, there are certain benefits you will get from joining one, regardless of which one it is. As mentioned earlier, you will be able to get advice and support on managing your BTL. This can even be in the form of telephone support, meaning that you can get quick replies and quick answers. Which is more effective than trying to figure it out yourself, and will save you from making mistakes that could cost you. These associations also analyse the legislation and prepare explanatory documents, so if there is anything that you don't understand or that is very complex, more

Chapter 1: What Makes a Good Landlord?

straightforward explanations will be available to you. You will also gain access to all legal documentation so that you do not have to go on the hunt for it yourself. Meeting like-minded people who are going through the same situations as you forms a great support structure that you can lean on. It can be just the helping hand you need to make property management much easier for you.

These are just a few of the benefits of joining a landlord association. You would have to go and do some research on specific landlord associations to see what they offer. If you are looking for a landlord's association to join in the UK, take a look at these options:

- Landlord's Guild
- Residential Landlords Association (RLA)
- National Landlords Association (NLA)

You are not required by the law to join an association, so at the end of the day it is your choice. They will support you regardless of how big or small your portfolio is. If you feel as though you are not getting anything from it, you are free to cancel your membership. For the benefits they offer, it is worth considering, at the very least.

Chapter 2: Getting Your Property Ready to Let

Your property is your business. It is what you will be using to attract tenants, and is the thing that you will need to protect and take care of. Before you allow someone to move in, you must have certain things in place to make sure it is safe to live. You will also need to decide what you want to provide in the house. As much as it would be great to just buy a house and move someone in immediately, it doesn't work that way. There are a few things you need to do and a few decisions you need to make before your property is ready to house tenants.

Maintaining Your Property and Keeping Your Tenants Safe

As a landlord, the responsibility falls on you to take care of the property and keep your tenants safe during their stay. If you do not follow the right steps or are negligent, you will be held liable for anything that goes wrong and will be fined. It is best to avoid this by knowing what your responsibilities are and how to go about doing them.

Houses in Multiple Occupation (HMOs) may have different requirements than what is stated here. These are places where you rent out the rooms to at least three different, unrelated people, and they share amenities such as the bathroom and kitchen. An HMO must have a licence if it is occupied by five or more people (a "large HMO") and the council can also include smaller HMOs for licensing. The council sets the regulations to follow and so it is best to contact your local authority and find out what is expected of you if you are running an HMO.

Gas and Electricity

If your property has gas installed in it, you must present the tenant with a gas safety certificate. This certificate must be given to them at the beginning of the tenancy. These checks should happen annually, and the new certificate must be handed to the tenant within 28 days of each check. This is imperative, as there are consequences to not doing this, such as not being able to evict your tenant with a Section 21 notice.

You should check all your electrical appliances and any electrical installations. You should run these checks every five years. Anyone who does electrical work or inspections on your property must be properly trained to do so. You must make sure that the person is qualified and reputable.

Carbon Monoxide and Smoke Alarms

These alarms are a must for any rental property. A check must be done on them to make sure they are working at the beginning of each new tenancy. You should let your tenant know that checks have been done on the alarms and that they are working. If you do not do this, you may be liable for a fine up to £5,000 under the Smoke and Carbon Monoxide Alarm (England) Regulations 2015.

Carbon monoxide alarms must be installed in all rooms that have appliances that run on solid fuel. This would include anything with an open fire or that is wood burning. Smoke alarms must be installed on every storey

Chapter 2: Getting Your Property Ready to Let

of the house. This is all to protect the tenant from any harm that may come if something were to go wrong with the appliances or anything else in the house.

Energy Efficiency

Privately rented properties are required to have an Energy Performance Certificate (EPC). This is received after the required checks have been done. The certificate must be given to the tenant of that property as soon as possible. The minimum rating a property should have is an E. This applies to all new rental properties and any renewals.

Landlords are responsible for the upgrades necessary should the property not meet the standard. To get the EPC rating up to E there are options available for third party funding so that you don't have to fund the upgrades yourself. Current avenues for third party funding are through the Energy Company Obligation, Green Deal Finance and the Renewable Heat Incentive.

If third party funding is not available, you don't have to pay for upgrades that will cost in excess of £3,500. If it is more than that amount to get to rating E, you will have to install improvements up to that limit and then can register for an exemption. If a tenant wants to perform any energy performance improvements on the property, they can ask your permission. You cannot refuse them without good reason. They are also allowed to have a smart meter installed if they are paying for the electricity bill themselves.

Water Safety

Of course, any rented property must have access to clean water, as well as a constant water supply. Although rare, you should also do a risk assessment on the water supply and be sure that there is no risk of Legionella. It is also the landlord's responsibility to make sure that the water is safe for the tenants.

HHRS

HHRS stands for the Housing Health and Safety Rating System. It is the measure that the council will use to determine whether a property is fit to be lived in. It does this by assessing the effect certain hazards could have on the occupants of the house (Basingstoke and Deane, n.d.). This was introduced under the Housing Act of 2004 (Ministry of Housing, Communities and Local Government, 2006).

Once you know what the hazards are, you are expected to remedy them to make sure the house is safe. It is worth noting that every property will have some sort of hazard and it would be nearly impossible to remove all of them. The ones that will be highlighted for change will be the ones that can cause serious health and safety issues.

To Furnish or Not to Furnish?

This is a common question. Many landlords struggle to decide whether they should rent out their property furnished or unfurnished. The truth is that there isn't just one answer. There are pros and cons to both. You have to take them all into account when deciding which option will be best for you.

Chapter 2: Getting Your Property Ready to Let

Renting Out a Furnished Property

When looking to furnish your property, you have to look at how much space you are working with. Smaller properties usually do better with being fully furnished, because they attract a particular type of tenant. Smaller properties, especially ones closer to the city, attract people who are not really looking for something permanent. The tenants that seek out a furnished property are generally not looking to stay in the area for an extended period of time. These types of people are usually long-stay tourists, people that have business in the city, students, or generally younger people.

If you are planning on furnishing your property, take the type of people you will attract into consideration. Try and go for younger, more modern pieces. Clean pieces that create a flow will work best. If you are a person who loves to design, then this could be an excellent project for you. Try and make it a comfortable space that you know someone would want to live in. You should also be aware that if you have opted to have your property furnished for your tenants, all furniture must be up to standard. Any required labels must be on the furniture, and they should all be fireproofed. Let's take a look at the pros and cons of renting out a furnished space.

There are some definite pros to renting out a furnished property. Firstly, you could charge higher rent. Generally, if someone is looking for a fully furnished property, they will be expecting to pay a bit more. You can also choose to decorate the space in such a way that it attracts higher-paying tenants. This is also dependent on where your property is situated. Buildings closer to cities or places with a lot of buzz might attract high-class business people. Designing your space in such a way that it looks high-end will allow you to tap into this market.

You would also be able to rent out a property much faster if it is furnished. People usually want to move in right away if they are seeking out a furnished property. There are also generally more people looking for furnished homes than ones looking for places they have to furnish themselves. If you are looking into short-term rentals, then this is the way to go.

Once the tenancy ends, the furniture still belongs to you. You have the option of using it for yourself or continuing to rent out the property with the furniture in it. Once you have bought the furniture, you are at liberty to do with it what you wish. Some people swap furniture between their rental properties so that there is always something new at each property. This will only work if you have multiple properties.

Another benefit is tax deductions. You would be able to deduct a percentage of the cost from your tax liability. Some of the expenses included are the replacement of a damaged item or the cost of disposal of an old item. Tax benefits in any context are always a win.

Moving onto the cons. One of the biggest cons with renting out a furnished property is that there is likely to be a higher turnover of tenants. When a tenant moves out, there is no guarantee that there will be another one lined up and waiting to move in. This puts you at risk of having the property vacant if you are not able to find a new tenant quickly.

Providing furniture in the property means that, if something breaks from wear and tear and can no longer be used, you will have to replace it. This is something you will have to factor into your budget, because you never know when this will happen. People tend to be more careless with things that aren't theirs, especially with younger tenants. You will also be responsible for the cleaning of upholstery and other items in between each tenancy.

Renting Out an Unfurnished Property

Just as furnished properties attract a certain type of person, so do unfurnished properties. The typical person that is looking for an unfurnished property is someone who has their own furniture and wants to bring that along. They are looking for a long term place to stay, and are typically older and may have kids. These types of people will probably be looking for a larger property, with enough room for the whole family. They are looking for a home, not just a place to stay for a short time.

Lugging around your furniture from place to place can be tiresome, so anyone with their own furniture is looking to plant somewhere and stay there. There are also pros and cons to unfurnished property, so take a look at them and consider if this is the right option for you.

Let's start with the pros. These tenants will be bringing over their own furniture, which means it is not your responsibility to insure it. If something breaks or needs to

Chapter 2: Getting Your Property Ready to Let

be replaced, that is at the tenant's cost, and you do not need to get involved. This definitely creates less admin for you, and there will be no money coming out of your pocket for these things.

These tenants will be staying for a long time, so that means that there is a lower risk of vacant periods. You will have a solid source of income for a good few years. Typically, there will be less management required from you. You will be responsible for certain things, but because this is someone's long term home, you don't have to be as involved as you would with a short term lease. Tenants also tend to be happier when they have their own items in their space. The home will feel like theirs, and they are more likely to take care of it as such.

Some of the cons you would have to consider for an unfurnished property is that the rent will be expected to be cheaper for it. You are offering nothing but the property itself, so you will have to charge accordingly. It might also take you longer to find someone to rent an unfurnished property since it is a long term commitment.

Chapter 2: Getting Your Property Ready to Let

Best of Both

If you are still having trouble deciding between the two, there is a middle ground. You could try a partially furnished property. This just means that you will provide some staple pieces of furniture, but just the necessities. Then, the tenant has the freedom of bringing in their own items to give it a more homey feel. On the other hand, if the tenants need to move in quickly, there is enough in the house to sustain them until they either bring over their own items or get around to purchasing some. Some of the items you could include would be large appliances such as a fridge, stove, and washing machine. If you do choose this route, then make sure the pieces you choose are of a neutral style. When tenants move in, they would want it to match what they have.

Adding a few key pieces gives you flexibility. If your tenants already have all their own furniture and appliances, then you can just put yours in storage for future use. Your property will be able to be marketed to a much wider audience, making it easier to find tenants. You should weigh up the cost of having furniture in storage versus any additional rental income from offering a furnished property to see if this is worthwhile.

At the end of the day, the choice is up to you. Take a look at your options and make a decision from there. Remember to take into account the size of your property, where it is situated, and the type of tenants you are trying to attract. It is also worth doing your research on the area just to see what the typical person living there is looking for. That could give you more information to base your decision off.

Checklist and Key Takeaways

- Make sure that your property has working smoke and carbon monoxide detectors in the required areas.
- You must do an annual gas safety check and receive a certificate from this. This certificate must be given to the tenant.
- You need to have an Energy Performance Certificate and have a rating above E.

Chapter 2: Getting Your Property Ready to Let

- All furniture supplied by you must be fireproofed and have the necessary labels.
- You must conduct a risk assessment on the water supply of the property for exposure to Legionella.
- Make sure that the property is free from any serious health and safety hazards.
- When you perform any checks, retain any proof and paperwork. You must be able to prove that these things were done. This will protect you from any potential fines and allow you to evict tenants in the future.
- Smaller properties do better when furnished because they attract students, singles, and young people.
- Larger properties do better when they are unfurnished because they are better suited for more established families who probably have their own furniture.
- You can get the best of both worlds by only buying a few key pieces. This will give you the flexibility to attract a wider pool of people.

Chapter 3: Marketing Your BTL

Marketing is a big part of property rental. It is what attracts people to your property in the first place. Most likely, you do not want to use a letting agent. In a time where the internet is a free resource, that is a smart move. Letting agents can charge quite high fees, so if you can do it yourself, then why not? All you need is a computer, a good internet connection, and know-how.

What Do You Have to Offer?

When you are marketing your property, the goal is to make it attractive. People need to want to move in there, so you need to take a look at your property and think about what is so great about it. As much as there are thousands of people looking for a home, there are also thousands of homes being advertised. Yours needs to be the one to stand out. The more people that are interested in your property, the greater chance you have of finding an ideal tenant.

Chapter 3: Marketing Your BTL

Find Your Target Audience

Before you even start marketing your property, you have to decide on your target audience. Not every property is made for every type of person. Think about it: when you are young and single, you are looking for something smaller that can cater to your basic needs, and you probably want something close to the fun, lively parts of the city. When you're older with a family, a suburban house with a garden is more ideal. Young couples will be looking for a smaller starter home, and business professionals will look for a place that is close to work and perhaps has room for a home office. Older, retired couples will be looking for a quieter area, and probably a smaller space.

Of course, you can't just pick one of these categories and shape your house accordingly. You need to see what you are working with. Take into account the size of the house, how many bedrooms, the location, and certain extras like a garden, and garages. All of these will play a factor. Also, take a look around the neighbourhood and see what kinds of people already live there. This will give you a good indication of who you will attract.

Chapter 3: Marketing Your BTL

Once you have decided on your target audience, you can market it accordingly. You can highlight the features that will attract that certain type of person. Marketing too broadly runs the risk of not attracting anyone. People will pass things by if they don't believe it will suit their needs. If you want to attract a family, highlight things that families would want, like a smaller, extra room that can be used as a playroom for kids. If you want to attract a business person, you can instead say that this space is perfect for an office. Making things like this clear will increase the chances of you finding the type of tenant you want, and who your property caters to best.

Be Descriptive

Your advert is the only thing people have to go on when they are searching on different platforms. They cannot see your property, so they have to be caught with the description of it. Yes, the visual aspect of photographs is important, but we will get to that a bit later.

When people are looking for a house, they are probably going through hundreds of listings. The ones that will peak their interests are the ones that will provide them

Chapter 3: Marketing Your BTL

with a full picture of what the house offers. If the advert says three bedrooms/two bathrooms, what makes it stand out from any other property of a similar standard? What makes the customer want to click to enquire on that listing? If there is nothing, then you will not get any results. Or, if you do get enquiries, they might not be of good quality. You want enquiries from the right people, who actually fit the demographic of the person you want to attract.

Now, you don't want to go over the top and add the square meters of every room with the exact tile colour, etc. It still needs to be easy to read. Put in the information that will add value and use a bulleted list. Bulleted lists are much easier to read and find information on. Your list could look something like this:

- Walking distance from a public transport pick-up station
- Three schools to choose from in the area
- Local attractions (tailor this to the type of person you want to attract)
- Front and back garden

- State whether it is furnished or unfurnished (give a breakdown of the items, if it does come with furniture)
- Number of bedrooms
- Number of bathrooms
- Low crime rates
- Number of garages

Add anything else that you feel makes your property stand out. This can be about the location, the house itself, or the benefits of living in that specific area. These details will be valuable in attracting your preferred tenant.

Be Flexible and Open to Incentives

Flexibility in terms of your standards could be the defining factor of whether you find a great tenant or not. Not many landlords are willing to accommodate pets or DSS tenants. By doing this, you will seriously limit your prospective pool of tenants.

Think about how many people have pets, and then how many properties you see that are pet-friendly. The numbers do not match up. That means there are a lot of people looking for places that will allow them to bring little Scruffy along with them. If you allow pets, it could be an opportunity to increase the rent, because your property will be in more demand.

Before you allow pets to live on your property, you must consider the type of pets and the type of space you have. Make sure that you market for the space you have. If you have a small apartment, you can say only small dogs and cats are welcome. Bigger properties can be a bit more liberal with this. It would also be wise to have a clause in the tenancy agreement that includes damages caused by the pet. Of course, if you are renting out an unfurnished property, then there won't be much for the pet to damage. You could also meet the pet before you allow the owner to rent, just to see if it is well behaved. There are always ways to work around these issues, and many times pets don't cause too much of a problem. It is worth considering being flexible with this.

Incentives are another excellent way to make your property more attractive, especially if you are struggling to find a tenant. If the market is oversaturated with similar properties, then you have to stand out in some way. Offering things like free wifi or utilities included might increase the interest in your property. Some landlords don't want to do this because they think it will be too expensive, but I guarantee it will be nowhere as expensive as having a void for months.

Take Photos

Not adding professional photos to your advert is probably the biggest mistake people make when marketing their properties. Whenever you search through the online portals, you will always see countless ads with no pictures, or really poor quality pictures. People only have the ads to go on when they are searching for a property, and the more information you give them, the more enticing it is. People are visual, and they want to be able to look at something before they move forward with enquiring about it.

It is a must to add photos to your marketing strategy. It really doesn't matter which platform you are using, even if it is just a tweet. Still, it is not just about putting any picture up there; it has to be good quality photos. You want to entice people into being interested in your property. If your photos are of poor quality, that is the

Chapter 3: Marketing Your BTL

kind of tenants you will attract. Your marketing should reflect the type of person you want to move into your property.

The best thing to do is to get a professional photographer in to help you. It may cost a little bit of money, but these pictures will be so valuable to your marketing campaign. Photographers will be able to use the right angles to make your room look more attractive. Using the wrong angles shrinks the room. Instead, you want your room to look big and spacious in photos. Just because you can take a good selfie doesn't mean you could be a professional photographer—trust me on this.

Your pictures should be clear and free from blur. Sharp images with sharp colours are what will attract the most people. Don't put your children or pets in the pictures, no matter how cute they are. It just isn't going to translate well. Having these in your photos will just look unprofessional, and may end up turning some people off your property. Remember, you are trying to highlight the features of the house. You are meant to be selling the property after all, so that is the only thing that should be in the photo. Clean up and make it look as neat and presentable as possible. You could even do a little more and move things around to enhance the space. Lastly, make sure you are taking the picture in daylight. Dull lighting will bring down the most beautiful spaces. Even artificial lighting is not comparable to natural light, so wait for the light to be at its brightest and get snapping.

Reaching Your Audience

When you market your property, you need to know where to do it. Luckily, there are various platforms which you can use to reach people who are in the market for a new home.

Online Portals

In the introduction to this chapter, I mentioned how you do not need to use letting agents, especially because they charge large fees. I am not going back on what I said here, so hear me out. The use of online letting agents is a great tool for private landlords because they reach a large audience. An online letting agent also does not charge the exorbitant fees that a regular letting agent does. The fees

Chapter 3: Marketing Your BTL

can be as little as £29 to advertise with OpenRent, which, compared to the £1000's you may be paying a standard letting agent, is a small sum.

Once you are registered with an online letting agent, you have access to all of their customers as well as the major online property portals. The two portals that stand out are Rightmove and Zoopla. These two alone get millions of views. This can drastically increase your chance of finding the right tenant, just based on the fact that the reach is so wide. It doesn't actually matter what type of tenant you're after; you are bound to get some enquiries from these two websites.

Other online platforms you could try are Gumtree, Facebook Marketplace, TheHouseShop, and social media in general. All of these are completely free, so if you can't spend any money in search of a tenant, you can try these. You can just pop your ad up and wait for someone to reply. Even just a tweet or a status update proves effective. You never know who is looking for a place to stay. The more platforms you use, the more people you will have who are interested. This will increase your chances of finding an ideal tenant.

Chapter 3: Marketing Your BTL

Viewings

Now that you have completed the first step in the process, which is getting your ad out there, it is time to move on to step two. You now have people interested in your property, and they want to see it in person. This process is just as important to you as it is to them. Sure they get to see if the place matches their standards, but you get to see if they match yours. This is the first time you will be meeting them, so use this as a time to weed out any potential problem tenants.

Before you get to the viewing process, there is one more thing I highly recommend you do, especially if you have lots of interested parties. Create a tenancy application form and get the prospective tenants to fill it in. We will go into more detail about these forms in the next chapter.

Now that you have received and gone through those application forms, you can go ahead and call in your chosen few to view the property. Be on the lookout for any telltale signs that this person is not going to be a good tenant. You may not think it is that big of a deal, but you can tell a lot about someone from the way they carry themselves, the way they dress, and even from their personal hygiene. If you feel uneasy about someone, then it is best to trust your gut.

You can have open viewings, where you set a time and just allow people to come in to see the house. Many agents do this type of open house format, but the problem with this is that it can be a waste of time. If you are a busy person, you want to be able to use your time in the most efficient manner. This might not be the way to do that. It does allow you to meet people straight off the bat, but the chances of you meeting people who are not well suited for the property are very high in this scenario.

As much as you will be checking your potential tenants, they are also checking out their potential home and landlord. So make sure the house is presentable, do a bit of cleaning, and make it feel as comfortable as possible. You can even go a step further and offer refreshments, such as water and a snack. You want to have someone who doesn't want to settle for just anything; these are the types of people that will take care of your property. Be friendly and presentable, and make sure to answer their questions the best you can. You should know your property, so be prepared for any kind of question. Understand how certain things work so if they ask you

you can tell them, and even demonstrate it to them. If you are knowledgeable about your property, it shows that you care for it and will indicate that you are willing to take care of it in the future if something needs fixing. Above all, just be honest. It is possible that they will ask something you have not even thought of. In this case, just say you are unsure but are willing to find out for them. Nothing is worse than someone waffling on or trying to divert the conversation. Never make empty promises. This is a reflection on the type of person you are.

Do not stop the viewing process until you have someone who has paid their deposit, and has signed the lease. I have settled on a tenant only to have that person pull out at the last minute. That leaves you in a position where you have to start all over again. That can be seriously frustrating. Continuing with the viewing process gives you a safety net. If the person suddenly drops out, then you can just continue the process until you find someone else. Also, if you have other people interested, it can be an incentive for the first prospective tenant to hurry up and make a decision.

Let's Talk About Rent

The mistake many landlords make is not asking for the right price. The amount of rent you ask for can be the factor that either gets you the right tenant or leaves your property vacant for too long. Of course, as a landlord, you want to limit the amount of time your property does not have a tenant. Take the time to really think about what your ideal rent is and make sure that it is justified.

If you ask for too little, you may find that people flock to your property. This may sound good, but you will be losing money in the long run. If your property is worth a certain amount, don't be scared to charge that amount. On the other hand, and this is a more common problem, don't charge too much. Oftentimes, landlords charge way too much because they believe their property is worth much more than what it is. This might be because they have put in a lot of work into the property and believe because of this the property is worth more. I can guarantee you that anyone looking for a house is not going to care about how much work it was for the landlord. They care about what they are going to pay, and what they are getting for that price.

Chapter 3: Marketing Your BTL

Taking all that into account, it still doesn't answer the question, "How much should I charge for rent?" Every property is different, and therefore will be worth a different amount. It is up to you to do your research to find out what the market value is. Figuring out how much other people are charging and what the going rate for a property similar to yours will allow you to make the best decision.

The portals that were mentioned before are not only for finding tenants. They can be a valuable tool for figuring out how much you should be charging. If you hop onto one of the portals like Rightmove and search for properties similar to yours, you will quickly see what the average asking price is. You could also go onto Gumtree, since they make direct sales and is not through an agent, and you can see what landlords expect to get. Also do your research on newspapers and on letting agent websites. You should try and get the broadest view on pricing. Just be cautious when you use a letting agent's website or call one for information; they often inflate prices because they work on a percentage commission. If the prices you are getting from them seem too good to be true and do not match any of your other research, then it

Chapter 3: Marketing Your BTL

is safe to assume the prices they are giving you are inflated to win your property listing.

Once you have accessed all of your portals, you must make sure the criteria for your searches are correct. You can't compare your two-bedroom apartment with one garage to a three-bedroom, two-bathroom apartment that has a garden. We have to compare apples to apples. Commodities also matter, so take that into account. Even if the properties are similar, there may be extra things that the other property has that can be used to drive up the price. Look out for features such as furnishings, garages, parking spaces, and garden space.

The area also matters when comparing properties. Look for properties in your area, as certain areas are in higher demand than others. You can find out this information by calling a letting agent and pretending to be a renter, saying that you are thinking about renting out a property in your area and enquiring about prices. They will be able to give you some insight into rental prices and whether the area is in demand or not. If the area is a high demand, you could increase your price, especially if there is a low supply of properties in the area.

Chapter 3: Marketing Your BTL

Once you have done all of this research and seen what the market has to offer, you can sit down and decide on what is reasonable for you to charge. If the average market value for similar properties is £900 per month, then it might be smart for you to charge £850 to make sure you get a tenant quickly. You want to price your property competitively, and not at the exact rate that everyone else is charging. If you keep it the same, then there is nothing making your property stand out. This could mean that you have to wait a much longer time before you get a tenant. In the long run, this will cost you more money than pricing a bit lower than what your competitors are asking. Plus, if your tenant feels like they are getting a good deal, they will want to stay longer. This will reduce the risk of voids and give you a steady profit.

Pricing is arguably the most important aspect when marketing your property. Making smart choices will allow you to get the best value for your property and be able to attract the right tenants. That's the major goal of being a landlord: attracting the right tenants.

Checklist and Key Takeaways

- Narrow down on your target audience and market your property specifically to them.
- Give as much valuable information in your advertisements as you can. You want your property to stand out.
- Be a little flexible when it comes to your criteria. You don't want to exclude a whole group of people based on something that can be worked around.
- Remember to take lots of high quality, property flattering, professional photos. It will substantially increase the interest in your property.
- Utilise as many online platforms as possible. The more you put your advertisements out there, the higher chance you have of finding the right tenant.
- Create an application form to help choose the best applicants from a large pool.
- Don't skip on the viewings. This is a good time to meet your prospective tenants.
- Be well-dressed and friendly, and make sure your house is neat and presentable.

Chapter 3: Marketing Your BTL

- Be fair when deciding on how much rent to charge. Charging too much will deter many great potential tenants, and charging too little means that you are shortchanging yourself.

Chapter 4: Selecting Tenants

Choosing the right tenant is crucial to the success of your BTL. The wrong tenant will make your life much harder, and might actually lose you money. It is much better to do the extra work in the beginning to save yourself from having to manage a bad tenant. Just remember that having certain standards is not grounds to be biased. You should never discriminate based on age, race, gender, or disability.

The two questions you have to keep in mind when picking a tenant are, "Can this person pay the bills?" and "Will they take care of the property?" If you cannot answer these questions with complete certainty, then you might have to move on and find someone new. We will be going through the best ways to filter through people and notice a bad tenant. These are the skills you will need to master to make your life as a landlord easier. You will always be looking for tenants; there are very few circumstances where a tenant will stay at the same property for extremely long periods of time. You never know when your tenants might leave, so you need to be skilled in the art of selecting a good tenant.

Chapter 4: Selecting Tenants

Processing Applications

The application process will ideally happen before the viewing process. Doing it this way will save you a lot of time chatting with and meeting people that have no chance of renting your property. Rather than spending all that extra time meeting people, get the application process done first. This works best if your BTL is in an in demand area, you can go through the applications and decide who you want to view the house. Some people just take chances when they apply, and it can be highly frustrating to have to meet these people and have them waste your time.

Before you are able to process the applications, you need to make an application form. The form can be tailored to your specific preferences, but there are a few things that should be standard. These are the tenant's details, the details of their current landlord, guarantor details, details of employment, details of all occupants, and any other extras like smoking status or pets. This will give you a good idea of if this person would be suitable as a tenant. For example, by getting employment details like salary, you would be able to see if this person would be able to

Chapter 4: Selecting Tenants

pay for their rent. Having these application forms will also help you to decide between tenants later on down the line.

You can get these details by asking them to complete a series of questions and to email responses to you before arranging the viewing, or you could take their responses over the phone and get the answers from them that way. Where there are fewer applicants, a phone call is often the best way because you will be able to see how this person engages over the phone and get a better idea of who this person is. Try to be as friendly and casual as possible. Making them feel comfortable will be the best way to tell how they are naturally. Don't be surprised if people don't want to fill out the application form or give you the information you require. This is actually pretty common. In most cases, you don't want these types of people to be your tenants anyway. They are either hiding something or are just going to be a person who complains about every little thing. Just say thank you for your time and move on.

Once you have all of your application forms ready, you must go through them. The goal here is not to just eliminate and pick the top one. All you want to do is

Chapter 4: Selecting Tenants

eliminate the ones who will not be a good fit. So, remove those who do not have a high enough salary to sustain the rent, have too many dependents for the size of your property, or are not willing to provide a guarantor. You can use your discretion here.

At the end of going through your applications, you should have as many applicants as possible to view your property. The reality is that not everyone who views your property is going to want to move in, so if you are too strict with the applications, you will be missing out on potential tenants. As long as there are no red flags and they meet your minimum requirements, give them a call to come in to view the property.

Once you have picked the ones you like, don't forget to reject the ones you didn't. You don't have to call them; an email should suffice (and in my opinion is the easiest way to reject people). It is just a common courtesy to do so, and it will save you from receiving calls and emails from candidates trying to follow up. Another way to go about this is to state clearly that if they do not hear back from you by a certain date, then their application has been unsuccessful. Then, at least they know where they stand after the date has passed.

Having these applications also allows you to have valuable information for all of your potential tenants. Down the line, it will be much easier for you to just pull out the application form for the information you need, rather than running after the person trying to find out their last name (or whatever other information you may need).

Tenant Referencing

This is undoubtedly one of the most important steps when finding a tenant for your property. Many landlords seem to skip over this step, and it usually does not turn out well for them. You will never know if someone is going to be able to pay their rent, take care of the property, and just be an overall good tenant until you check their history. Never skip this step! Unfortunately, you really can't trust people on their word, no matter how nice they are or how much you get along with them.

At the end of the day, you will be the one to lose out if your let to a terrible tenant. That is why you have to do everything in your power to make sure you pick a reliable

Chapter 4: Selecting Tenants

person. A few things you will have to check to make sure the prospective tenant is a good fit are:

- A credit check
- Past landlord reference
- Employment history and salary (if the tenant can afford the rent)
- The tenant's Right to Rent

You will need to do a credit check so that you can see the tenant's full credit history. You will be able to see if they have been blacklisted, gone bankrupt, or have bad credit. Credit history is important because it shows how the person handles their money, and if they can pay their bills. This is one of the most important of the checks, and you will need the prospective tenant's consent before doing it. It will need to be done through a third-party provider such as NRLA.

Past landlord references are also really important. For this, the tenant will have to give you the name and contact details of current or past landlords. This is essentially the same process as calling for references when an employee gets a new job. It is done to check if the past landlord was happy with the tenant, if they took care of the property, and if they paid on time. The chances are if they didn't do these things for the past landlord, they will not do it for you.

When you do an employment history check, you are looking for a stable job and income. Their salary will indicate whether they will be able to pay the rent. You can also request the contact details of their employer and do a reference check there. The employer will be able to tell you if this person is trustworthy, how long they have worked at the company, and give a general character testimonial.

The last one on the list is the Right to Rent. This one is required by law. You have to check whether the prospective tenant can legally rent in the United Kingdom. This is the only one that is not optional for you to do and must be done for all occupants of the property who are over the age of 18, regardless if they are the one who is responsible for the rent. If someone is a British citizen, then they will be able to rent, but you are not allowed to discriminate by deciding for yourself who you should check and who not to. Beware that you can get an unlimited fine or be sent to prison for renting your property to someone who fails the right to rent checks and is not allowed to stay in England (Gov.UK, n.d.). You

Chapter 4: Selecting Tenants

do this check by asking your tenants to view the original documents that prove that they have the right to live and work in the UK. Make sure to take a copy and keep on file with the date you made the check.

The law does not state that you have to do these checks (except for the Right to Rent check). It is up to the landlord's discretion. However, if the prospective tenant refuses to consent to these checks being done, you are well within your rights to refuse to move forward with the process.

If you have received any bad references and you are not comfortable with the results of the checks you have done, you can deny the application. In this case, if a holding deposit was given to you, you must return it to them within seven days of you making the decision to not proceed with the process (Propertymark, n.d.). If any information the prospective tenant gave you was false or misleading, you can then withhold the deposit. This must then be communicated in writing to the prospective tenant, and the reasoning for the deposit being withheld must be clearly stated.

The only cost you need to incur for doing these reference checks is to pay for the credit check and this can be from

£6 to £25 depending on the supplier you use. For everything else, the tenant should provide you with all the documents you need. Note that you cannot ask the tenant to pay for referencing checks in England, Wales, or Scotland. Your costs of doing these checks will be much less than those you could have by letting to a tenant who cannot afford the rent.

Avoiding Bad Tenants

We have talked about ways in which you can find a good tenant, but what about avoiding bad ones? If we are too focused on trying to find the aspects that will indicate a good tenant, we will miss the telltale signs of a bad one. Unfortunately, there is no shortage of bad tenants, and you do not want them in your property. Prevention is always better than cure, so make sure you are doing everything you can to notice a bad tenant before it is too late in the process.

The points that are listed here have been red flags for many landlords, but that does not mean you have to follow this religiously. Rather, use it as a guide and stop,

Chapter 4: Selecting Tenants

think, and ask yourself questions when you come across someone with one of these qualities. They may have perfectly good explanations for whatever it is, so be careful that you are not losing out on a great tenant because you are too intolerant.

Be Cautious of Cash Payers

Sometimes people will offer to pay you rent in advance with cash. They will want to drop a large amount of rent, maybe about six months' worth. This may seem like the ideal situation. I mean, you don't have to worry about your tenant paying rent for six months! Just be careful. This could be a sign that this person does not want you to bother them for the six months so that they can do something dodgy with the property (maybe even something illegal). Don't rule this out. People are really not what they seem, and you don't want to be involved with anything like this. The other, more common reason they want to pay upfront is that they have bad credit or rental history, and they are trying to divert you.

Now, there are cases where people will want to pay upfront for legitimate reasons, so don't automatically rule them out. Just make sure you do the necessary background checks. You just want to make sure that this person will be able to sustain the rent after the six months (or however long they have paid upfront,) and that they don't have a history of suspicious behaviour. Ask them questions to why they want to pay upfront and see if you can pick up anything from their answers. If they start getting defensive, then this could also be a red flag. Keep your eyes open and use your discretion.

Don't Just Accept the First Person Who Is Interested

You might be tempted to take the first person that wants to rent the property. Don't fall into this trap! It is true that the longer the property remains vacant, the more it will cost you, but in the long run a bad tenant will cost you so much more. Make sure you go through the process, even if it delays the renting and payment process. Jumping the gun is one of the worst things you can do. Even if the process might seem long and tedious, better to be sure than leave anything up to chance and end up regretting it later.

Chapter 4: Selecting Tenants

Say No If You Have To

Saying no or rejecting people can be tough for some people, especially if you don't like conflict or confrontation. The truth is that if you are going to be a landlord or a boss of any kind, you will have to get used to dealing with confrontation and handling it well. It comes with the territory, unfortunately.

If you are having doubts for some reason, then there is no point in continuing on and wasting both of your time. You are not obligated to do anything or sign the papers, regardless of how far you are in the process (of course, if you have already signed the contract, then it's a different story). Even deposits can be reversed, so don't feel as though you have to take this person. If new information comes up that makes you uncomfortable, then you are free to reject the person. I would advise that you do not accept deposits or sign contracts until you have done all the checks you need to.

The best way to handle a person you do not want to move forward with is to tell them that there are many other interested parties, so you will have to finish with the process and get back to them. This way, you are not setting them up or lying to them. You will be seeing other prospective tenants, even if they are not yet in the pipeline. Always continue with the application process until you are sure you have a tenant, meaning the person has signed the contract, paid you, and is moving in. If all of these have not happened, then continue seeing potential tenants. You can't trust anyone at their word. Even if they say they are going to move in, they can change their mind, and you will be the one left with nothing.

Always Take a Deposit

Don't be swayed by people's words. It doesn't matter how sweet they sound. You have to have the deposit in your bank account before you move forward. Even if they want to pay in instalments, it is a red flag. Think about it: if someone is looking for a place to stay and has a good financial situation, why wouldn't they be able to pay the deposit in full? If they are already struggling to come up with the money at the beginning, there is no way to be sure that this won't continue throughout the tenancy. Also, instalments could lead to legal complications, and

Chapter 4: Selecting Tenants

you don't want to deal with that. You want everything to run as smoothly as possible.

Take Note of Mannerisms

This one could come across as judgemental, but I can promise these things matter. Sometimes the reference checks are not enough to go on. You have to consider the person standing in front of you. Everything about a person will tell you something about them, so look for the subtle hints. In many cases, you can trust your gut. There are sometimes little things that make someone seem a bit off to you. In my experience, your gut is usually right. Don't feel as though you are too judgmental if you can't shake the feeling.

Let me give you some examples of subtle things that can be picked up on. The way a person dresses is the first one. First impressions do matter, so if they are not willing to dress up a little, then they clearly don't care. It's not about dressing fancy, but rather showing respect to the person you are going to see and trying to make a good impression on them. The second thing to be wary of is someone who haggles about the rent. Now, it is perfectly

Chapter 4: Selecting Tenants

ok for them to ask for a lower price and make a lower offer. People want to get the best deal, and that is understandable. Where it becomes a problem is when they keep pushing after you have shown no interest in going lower, or if they make a ridiculously low offer. It could be an indication that this person may not be able to pay the amount that you are asking.

The third thing you should watch out for are people who are not considerate of your time. These will be people who arrive late (or not at all) to viewings or are constantly rescheduling meetings. If they have a good reason and have let you know in advance, then that is perfectly fine. However, when they just don't arrive or show up late with a weak excuse, you should proceed with caution. These types of people could be the ones to pay their rent late or "forget to tell you something broke." They are unreliable and inconsiderate. Do you want someone like that on your property? Of course, use your discretion here, because there could be good reasons for rescheduling or not showing up. Most of the time, however, you can tell if someone is being genuine or is making up a story.

Chapter 4: Selecting Tenants

Inaccurate or Missing Information

This is another area in which your tenant application form will come in handy. The tenant will have filled out all the necessary information on the application form, but when you do their reference checks, make sure to check back with their original application forms. Sometimes people will place things on initial forms or even tell you things that you want to hear, but they end up not being true. Honesty is going to be so important for a tenant and landlord relationship, so if they have already started out by lying, it is not a good sign.

Even if there is missing information on any forms that you have given them, this could also be a signal to you. I mean, if the person could not even be bothered to fill out the form properly, it says a lot about them. Maybe they are really not interested in renting out the property, in which case it would be a complete waste of your time to continue with the screening process. Or maybe they were just too lazy to fill it out or didn't understand something on the form, so rather just left it out. These forms are usually not too difficult, and if they really were stuck they could have gotten a hold of you to get some clarity. If

Chapter 4: Selecting Tenants

someone is too lazy to fill out a form correctly, then I highly doubt they will be motivated enough to take care of your property if you make them your tenant.

Don't Place Too Much Value on Status

We can all fall into the trap of placing someone on a pedestal because of their position in society or their job title. That is why so many people throw their title around. A doctor or lawyer automatically gets more respect when they reveal what they do for a living. As much as you can respect the person because they have worked hard and are now in a very high up position, don't use this as the deciding factor of whether this person will make a good tenant or not.

You do want people who earn a good salary and are stable; this is one of the things you should be looking for when vetting tenants. The only problem is that it can cause a smokescreen, and then you will miss other red flags. Just because someone has a great job or has high social standing, that doesn't make them a great tenant. Just keep your eyes open when dealing with people with status. Make sure you don't abandon all your other criteria because of it.

Check Their Communication Skills

The way someone speaks and carries themselves will tell you a lot about them. If the person struggles to answer simple questions, that may be an indication that they are hiding something. You don't want to judge too harshly on something like this, but you do want someone who will be able to communicate with you clearly when you enquire about something regarding your property. You also want someone who will be open and honest if you do accept them as a tenant, so if they can't give you straight forward answers to your questions now, there is no certainty that they will in the future.

You can also do a quick scan of their social media. I mean, if employers can do it, so can you. What someone posts reveals what they value and what kind of person they are. If they have lots of pictures that show all they do is drink and party, that might be grounds to take a step back and think if this person will be responsible enough to take care of your property.

Chapter 4: Selecting Tenants

Look at Their Previous Rent

Having a look at how much they used to pay for rent will show you how much they have set aside for rent. If there is a big jump between what they used to be paying and what you expect them to pay, you should find out why they are willing to make that jump. It could be a case where they need a place to stay in a hurry, so at the moment they are ok with the big price gap, but in the future they might not be. They could have also not thought it through enough, so they believe that they will be able to pay the new amount.

If a tenant is not happy with how much rent they pay, it could lead to them becoming troublesome down the line. Rather than letting it get to that point, ask them why they are willing to make a steep rent jump. You can tell if they are prepared for it by their answer. If they say they have received a salary increase or have been saving for a nicer place, then by all means take them on. However, if they are not able to give a clear answer or the answer does not sound well thought through, you should be careful.

Chapter 4: Selecting Tenants

Checklist and Key Takeaways

- Start by making an application form and giving it to each prospective tenant to fill out. Application forms will hold valuable information for you to use in the future.
- Go through all the application forms and decide which applicants you would like to come in to view the house.
- Make sure to conduct tenant referencing and that they have the right to live and work in the UK. You can never trust people on their word. Background checks are essential.
- Background checks don't reveal all about a person. Keep your eye out for any red flags when you meet prospective tenants and throughout the whole process.
- Take note of the little things when you meet the potential tenants in person. Sometimes a person's mannerisms say more about them than the reference checks.

Chapter 4: Selecting Tenants

- Don't be too harsh. Always ask to see if there is a reasonable explanation for something you deem a red flag.
- If you have a bad feeling about someone, you are probably right. Trust your gut. It will save you from uncomfortable situations in the future.

Chapter 5: Tenancy Agreements

There are a lot of legal aspects to renting out a property. If you want to be successful in this business, you must know and understand what is required of you. All documents, agreements, and policies are there to protect the landlord and the tenant. Failure to comply with any mandatory steps can result in some large fines for the landlord.

Agreements and Assured Shorthold Tenancy

Assured Shorthold Tenancy (AST) is the most common tenancy agreement. Almost all rental contracts between tenants and private landlords fall into this category. If your tenancy began after February 28th, 1997 (I think it's safe to assume that if you are reading this book, it does), then it will most likely be an AST (The Landlord, n.d.-a). Bear in mind that if you have a lodger, that does not fall under an AST. A lodger is defined as someone who lives

Chapter 5: Tenancy Agreements

on the same property as you and shares common areas like a bathroom and kitchen. If you have a lodger, then you would have to sign a lodger agreement with them.

Although an AST agreement can be used in most circumstances, there are some situations they cannot. These are if the rent is over £100,000 a year, or if the rent is very low at about £250 a year, or £1000 a year if the property is in London (Gov.UK, n.d.-c). It can also not be classified as an AST if it is a holiday let, if the landlord is a council or government department, or if it is a business tenancy. For these cases, there are different agreements that need to be made and the contracts would defer to a regular tenancy.

There are various places where you can get a tenancy agreement from. Just make sure that the supplier is reputable. Many times, landlords will quickly download a free tenancy agreement from the web, and it will either be out of date or have clauses that are not enforceable by the law. A tenancy agreement is there to protect both you and your tenant. It can be a costly mistake to sign one that is not compiled correctly. The general rule should be if it is free, it is probably not going to meet the proper standards. Find somewhere that has some legal backing

Chapter 5: Tenancy Agreements

and experience to purchase your contracts from. It might save a lot of time and money down the line.

It is not stipulated by the law that the agreement has to be written down on paper, but it is highly advised. And by highly advised, I mean please do it! As soon as a landlord agrees on terms and conditions and the tenant moves in, both parties are protected by the legally binding lease terms. The problem arises when there is a dispute and there is not proof of what was agreed upon. It becomes very difficult to prove what was said and who is right. If it is written down, you both can go back to the agreement and see what was agreed upon in the first place. Therefore, any disputes can be handled diplomatically and with evidence. Signing a written agreement is for both of your protection and will lead to fewer problems in the future.

The length of the tenancy is really up to you and the tenant. However, the tenant does have the legal right to stay in the property for at least six months (The Landlord, n.d.-a). Usually, tenancy agreements last for 6 to 12 months. It is advisable to go no longer than this. If a problem arises, the tenant could make life very difficult for you, because it will be hard to get them out of the

Chapter 5: Tenancy Agreements

property before the tenancy is up. If you and your tenant are happy and want to continue with the tenancy, you can always renew it. Neither of you are losing out if you choose a shorter tenancy, it just provides some protection for you.

Both of you should have a copy of the tenancy agreement. This way, you both have quick access if you need to check something or need proof of something stated in the contract. Every person whose signature is on the contract should have a copy. This is a general rule that should be followed for all contracts. When it comes to signing the contract, I use digital signing software such as DocuSign and email the tenancy agreement to my tenants for signing, which saves me a visit to the property for tenancy renewals. They can then download the signed agreement for saving to their computer or print to file away.

As to what should be in the contract, it can vary in size depending on how much information you decide to put in it. There should be a few basic things included, such as the agreed-upon rent and when it is to be paid. The deposit should also be stipulated in the contract. The terms of tenancy and any obligations for both the landlord and the tenant should be clearly stated. The

Chapter 5: Tenancy Agreements

contract should also state things like that the property should not be left unattended for more than three weeks without letting the landlord know, that the property is only allowed to be used for residential purposes and that the tenant should not be a nuisance to neighbours and others around them. These are the basics of what should be included in a contract. Any finer details should be worked out between the parties involved. It is usually better to have a longer, more comprehensive contract, as there is more protection with that. Anything that is too vague or too lenient could lead to problems in the future. Although you do have the freedom to add clauses to the contract, everything you or the tenant add must comply with the law. Neither of you can put down things that are too restrictive, or that infringe upon basic rights. If it is not enforceable by the law, it will not hold up in court.

Either party is allowed to amend or improve the contract as long as the other party agrees to it. This can be done at any point during the existing contract. Any modifications or new conditions should be written down. You can either write up a whole new document that states the changes being made, or you can just amend the original contract. Make sure that it is signed and dated with the date the changes were agreed upon. If the original contract was a

Chapter 5: Tenancy Agreements

verbal one, you can also make the amends verbally, as long as there is proof of this. This can be in the form of witnesses or a notable performing of the new action. Again, it is wise to have all contracts and changes documented in writing and dated. It is also advisable to seek out legal advice before you amend a contract. You must be sure that whatever you are changing is enforceable by the law. If not, then any changes will be void. Plus, if there is a dispute that is taken to court, there will be no protection for you, even if the contract states something in your favour.

Landlords and tenants are still expected to perform and uphold basic obligations, even if it is not stipulated in the contract. As a landlord, it will always be your responsibility to take care of the property and perform basic repairs and upkeep. The tenant must take care of the property by not purposefully damaging anything, and looking after everything that is in the property. The tenant has a right to live on the property without being constantly bothered by the landlord. They should have quiet enjoyment of the property, and the landlord should keep their distance. These are the basic rights for both the landlord and tenant.

Chapter 5: Tenancy Agreements

Guarantors

It is smart for a landlord to request that their tenants have a guarantor. A guarantor is someone who will be liable to pay the rent of the tenant, should the tenant not be able to pay. Making sure your tenant has one will provide you with security if something does happen and the tenant is unable to pay you the money they owe.

The tenant will be able to pick a person whom they would like to be their guarantor. This person will have to consent to this. You can state this in your contract, and then if there is some point where the tenant does not pay, you can legally expect payment from the guarantor. The relation to the tenant does not matter. It can be a friend, cousin, parent, or sibling, as long as they sign their consent.

You should do a credit check on the guarantor the same way you should do one on the tenant. This is to make sure that this person will be able to pay the rent if they are required to do so. A guarantor must be between the ages of 18 and 75 and be a UK resident. If they meet all of these criteria, then you can accept them as your tenant's guarantor.

Taking Inventory

An inventory is basically a list that states the items present in the house when the tenant moves in and the condition each item is in. It is important to have an inventory list so that you have something to go back to when doing inspections. Not only that, but if the tenant breaks something, you have proof that it was not in the condition you left it. If there is no proof, the tenant can easily say that the item was in that condition when they got it, which means you will not be compensated for it. It will also protect the tenant from being unfairly accused of damaging something.

You can use an agent to do the inventory for you. If you go this route, the agent will guide you in terms of what to do. If you are going to do it yourself, then you should set a date to go over the inventory with the tenant. This can be on the date the tenant moves in or slightly before if the property is fully ready. The tenant should not be already

Chapter 5: Tenancy Agreements

moving in when you compile the inventory. You don't want items to be confused, and both parties need to agree about the condition of the items before the tenant moves in.

Formulate a list with all the items on it and the quality of these items. This list should include furniture and anything that comes with the property like sinks, walls, flooring. Basically, anything that has the potential to be damaged should feature on your inventory list. You can use your own rating system, but stating "poor", "moderate", or "excellent" when rating the items should work fine. There should also be a column where you describe the item in words, colours, size, and anything else you can use to describe the item. Next, you will need to have visual proof of the items. Since everyone's definition of what good condition is can differ, it is important to show how the item looked in the first place. Make sure you use a high-quality camera to take pictures of the items. If the photos are grainy or blurry, it is really not going to help you out. Do your best to take the photos in bright, natural light. This will result in much clearer pictures. Make sure the photos are dated, too. The best way to do this is to print them out, write the date, and sign each photo. You can also use video instead of photos.

Chapter 5: Tenancy Agreements

This can be easier if you want to get the full view of the item. To make it easier to run through the inventory list, make sure that the video shows the items in order of how they show up on the list.

Once both parties are happy with the inventory list and the photos/videos that accompany it, you can both sign the list. Both parties should have a dated and signed copy of this list, as well as dated and signed copies of all photos and videos taken. Keep digital copies of the pictures, since the physical photos may get destroyed or lost somehow. If this happens, you still want some sort of proof. You should redo the inventory lists every time there is a new tenant or whenever you renew a tenancy agreement. Even though this may seem tedious, you don't want to be out of money if something were to go wrong.

Your inventory list should be cross-checked every quarter when you go in for inspections. If there are any signs of damage, you will need to talk to your tenant about it. If it turns out that they have damaged the property in any way, they will need to pay for the damages. Upon a tenant moving out, you should also do an inspection and cross-check with your inventory list. Only perform this final inspection once the tenant has removed all of their items from the property. During the moving out process, a lot of things could potentially be damaged, and you don't want these to be overlooked. The tenant should be there for the final inspection and you should discuss any damages with them. It is also important to note that you will not be able to charge the tenant for general wear and tear. Everything does wear with use, so the tenant cannot be liable for this. You will not be able to charge the tenant for the replacement of a sofa when the colour has faded through months of use. These things will happen, so you should be fair when conducting inspections.

If damages occur and you and your tenant cannot agree on the damages and the costs thereof, then it should be escalated. The tenant's deposit should be in a holding scheme, and that scheme will handle it with a service called Alternative Dispute Resolution. Take pictures of the items, obtain the estimates, and inform your tenant that you will be contacting the scheme. The scheme's decision will be final. If you are deemed the right party, the money will be paid to you from the tenant's deposit. If the deposit does not cover the damages, the tenant is liable for the excess. If you do not want to go through the scheme, then it must be escalated to the court. This can be a lengthy process, so bear that in mind. However, sometimes it is inevitable, especially if the tenant does not want to pay.

Taking a Deposit

We have just spoken about how any damages can be paid for using the tenant's deposit, but in order for this to happen, the tenant needs to have made the deposit. A deposit creates security for the landlord, as it is some extra money that can be used in situations like this. There is no legal requirement that states you must take a deposit—it is just wise to do so.

The amount of money you can ask from your tenants for a deposit will depend on the amount of rent they pay. Usually, a non-pet-friendly rental property can expect at least four weeks of rent, and a pet-friendly one can expect five or six weeks of rent as the deposit. However, you should adhere to the tenant fees act. If the annual rent of the property is £50,000 or below, then the landlord may only ask for a maximum of five weeks of rent as a deposit. If the annual rent is above £50,000 and up to

Chapter 5: Tenancy Agreements

£100,0000, the landlord can ask for a maximum of six weeks rent (The Landlord, 2020c).

If you have decided to take a tenant's deposit, you must place it in a tenancy deposit protection scheme. This would need to be done within a 30-day period of receiving the deposit. There are three government-backed schemes in England and Wales; Deposit Protection Service, MyDeposits and Tenancy Deposit Scheme. Even if you are using a letting agent, it will be your responsibility to make sure the tenant's deposit is protected in a holding scheme. If you fail to protect the deposit, you might be liable to your tenant for three times the amount of the deposit.

The holding scheme will hold the tenant's deposit and then release it when the tenancy comes to an end. The deposit will be returned to the tenant within ten days of the tenancy ending. If there has been another agreement in which the deposit is to be given back to the tenant for a specific reason, the agreed amount will be returned within ten days.

Chapter 5: Tenancy Agreements

Documents to Give the Tenant

As a landlord, you will be required to have a few certificates for your property in order to rent it out. The first is a Gas Safety Certificate or CP12 certificate covering any gas appliances in the property you are renting out. This certificate must be renewed every year, and a copy must be provided to your tenant within 28 days from the date of inspection or at the start of their tenancy. Appliances owned by the tenant aren't your responsibility although you do need to ensure the safety of any connecting flues.

In addition to the Gas Safety Certificate, you should also provide the same for electrical equipment. The Electrical Safety Standards in the Private Rented Sector (England) Regulations 2020 require the electrical installations in the property to be inspected and tested every five years and for the inspection report to be given to the tenant within 28 days from the date of the inspection and electrical testing or at the start of the tenancy.

Another certificate you should have is an Energy Performance Certificate. This certificate only needs to be renewed every ten years. This certificate indicates the property's energy efficiency rating. If the property has a rating in the F and G bands, it will not be able to be let out. A copy of this certificate also needs to be given to the tenant.

In the case of tenants from abroad, make sure you have done a Right to Rent check discussed above under referencing. Do this check at least a month before they sign the papers to move in. You are required to check immigration status and that of any adults living with the primary tenant.

Checklist and Key Takeaways

- Make sure you get your tenancy agreements from reputable sources, and that all clauses are compliant with the law.
- Anything you sign must be signed by the tenant as well. Documents should be dated and each party should have a copy.

Chapter 5: Tenancy Agreements

- Have your tenant pick a guarantor with a good credit record, who will consent to paying any money due to you if the tenant is unable to.
- Compile a comprehensive inventory list that is accompanied with visual proof, either via photos or videos.
- The inventory list should contain furniture as well as any other items that form part of the house (sinks, mirrors, cabinets, etc.)
- If you take a deposit, it is your responsibility as the landlord to protect it by using a scheme.
- You must present the tenant with a Gas Safety Certificate and an Energy Performance certificate.
- It is the landlord's responsibility to check the immigration status of potential tenants and perform a Right to Rent check.

Chapter 6: Managing Your BTL

You have finally made it past the vetting process and have chosen your lucky tenant. Now you can start managing your BTL. This is the moment you have been waiting for: you will be collecting your first month's rent, and your tenant can move in. Let's get into how you can handle managing your BTL correctly from the moment you hand over the keys to the tenant.

Handing Over the Keys

This is not just a simple handing over of the keys. There are a few things you will have to get done before you can do this. You want the process to be smooth and hassle-free, but you also want to make sure you have covered everything and that there are no misunderstandings. This is the perfect time to have a chat with your new tenant and show them around one final time. Once you hand over the keys, you don't want to have to keep coming back or continuously having to take phone calls from the tenant. Make sure that you both have cleared up anything that needs to be cleared up so that they can enjoy their home and you don't have to worry.

Before you even get to the point of handing over the keys, all paperwork has to be done and signed. This should never be left to the last minute—the sooner the better. Also, the deposit and first month's rent should be paid. If the tenant delays on any one of these, then you should delay on the handing over of keys. It can get really complicated to have to get a deposit or try and get documents signed after the tenant has moved in, and you do not want those complications.

If you have not already gone through the inventory, then you can do so now. Go through the house and check that everything that is supposed to be there is there, and both of you should sign the inventory document. Remember to make the inventory list as descriptive as possible. This will help you if there ever is a dispute. Walk through the whole property, both the inside and the outside. Make sure you agree on everything, and any questions or concerns should be aired.

This is the time you will go through all the little things. Check meter readings and test locks and alarms. Give the tenant copies of instruction manuals and safety instructions for anything that needs it. They should be able to deal with simple problems by themselves and not have to call you for everything. You should also show the tenant that all appliances and electronics are working and make them sign for this. All this may seem like a lot, but it will be for both of your protection. This way, no one will be able to accuse the other of something they did not do or provide.

Once you have gone through the house and both parties are happy with everything, you can hand over the keys. You should hand over a set of keys for every person mentioned on the contract, so if there are two adults living in the house then both should be given a set of keys. If everything goes smoothly, the only time you should next be visiting the property is for inspections.

Maintaining the Property

After the tenant has moved in, all minor repairs and changes are their responsibility. So if they need to change a lightbulb or change the batteries in a smoke detector, this becomes their job. All major repairs will still be your responsibility. These repairs are that of the structure of the property, any major bathroom amenity (toilet, sink, etc.), general heating and water systems, and any damages that occur while conducting repairs (Gov.UK, n.d.-b).

Your property must remain in good condition throughout the duration of the tenant's stay. If you have to enter the property to make repairs, you are still required to give the tenant at least 24 hours' notice, unless it is an emergency. Your tenant can stay on the property as the repairs are being done, but just make sure to communicate to them if it would be dangerous for them to be in a certain area.

Damages caused by things like fires, floods, or any natural disaster cannot be charged to the tenant. You can rebuild and repair if you wish, but that would be at your own expense. If for any reason the property cannot be lived in while the repairs are being done, the tenant will have to temporarily move out. Before you can ask the tenant to leave, you both have to have a written agreement stating when the tenant can return, how long the repairs will take, and the details of alternative accommodations for the tenant (Gov.UK, n.d.-b). You may have to apply at court to get an order for your tenants to leave, and they will be more willing to grant this to you if you have provided another place for the tenant to live for the time being.

The tenant will be able to claim for a rent abatement if there are large repairs or renovations taking place. This will get them a reduction on their rent, and the amount of the reduction will depend on how much of the property is disrupted and cannot be used during the course of the repairs. If you have made improvements on the property, you may be able to increase the rent, but this all depends on the tenancy agreement.

Collecting Rent

Collecting rent should be the easiest part of the process because it is just the handing over of money, but unfortunately there are many cases where rent is paid late or not even paid at all. This is a major problem, and you need to know how to deal with it if you do get a tenant who is either a late payer or has not paid at all.

Chapter 6: Managing Your BTL

The best way to deal with rent payments is to ask your tenant to set up direct debit payments to you through GoCardless. It is an easy way to collect your rent on time, and the tenant does not have to do anything after the direct debit instruction is in place. If the tenant has cancelled a direct debit, you will be notified immediately by GoCardless and can call them to find out why. Having a direct debit will drastically reduce late-payments and the admin involved with processing payments. GoCardless charges 1% + £0.20 per transaction at the time of writing, which is a small fee for peace of mind, in my opinion.

There may be a case where your tenant is just not paying rent. This is not the ideal situation, but you should be prepared for it. The first thing you need to do is to make sure you are calm and don't overreact. You will need to get in contact with your tenant, and any outbursts or harsh reactions could make the situation worse. There could be a perfectly good explanation for this, and you don't want to jump to conclusions. Calling your tenant is best, since it is a more personal interaction and you can show the tenant that you are not angry, but rather just enquiring as to what is going on. After the phone call, send them an email or letter so that you have written proof of the correspondence. This is easier to keep track of than what was said over a phone call.

Hopefully, the tenant has just forgotten and will pay the rent immediately. If the tenant is having issues with finances, then you may be able to work out a payment plan. Try and be as courteous as you can with your responses, since this will probably be a sensitive topic for your tenant. If your tenant has a guarantor, you can request any outstanding payment from them. If you haven't been paid after 14 days of the initial conversation, then contact them again, preferably with a letter or email.

After two months, if the tenant has not made any effort to make a payment plan or communicate with you, you can legally begin the eviction process. Keeping the situation away from the court will be the best thing, since escalating it could mean extra costs for both you and the tenant. Explain this to them and see if they are willing to surrender the tenancy so that you can save yourself a lot of time and admin. Otherwise, you can serve a section 8 notice, which will give the tenant 14 days to remove themselves from the property (Propertymark, n.d.-b). The tenant may decide to take you to court, but if you have proof of all your correspondence and show that you did give the tenant the chance to pay the rent, you have a greater chance of evicting the tenant.

If the tenancy ends and there is still money owed, contact the tenancy deposit scheme you used. You may be able to deduct the outstanding money from the deposit. This is why it is so important to follow all the steps in the process. Not doing so could put you in a bad position, and you will be the one to lose out.

Checklist and Key Takeaways

- Make sure that all paperwork is done, contracts have been signed, and any money owed has been paid before you hand over the keys to the tenant.
- Use the handover time to go through the house and inventory list. You should both agree to everything and sign.
- Make sure everything is in working order and that there is written consent to this.
- You will still be responsible for any major repairs or renovations on the property.

Chapter 6: Managing Your BTL

- If there are any major repairs or renovations to be done, you may have to organise alternate accommodations for your tenant.
- Renovations may impact the rent for both you and your tenant. Be aware of what the tenancy agreement says regarding this.
- Tenants that have not paid rent need to be handled with care. Any unreasonable conduct from your side will not hold up well in court, should you need to escalate the situation.
- Make sure you keep a written record of all your communication between you and the tenant regarding unpaid rent.
- If the tenant has not paid rent in two months, you may start the eviction process.

Chapter 7: Ending the Tenancy

The chances of you being able to keep the same tenant indefinitely are extremely unlikely. Well done if you do! More likely, you will be dealing with ending a tenancy multiple times while managing your BTL and will need to know how to handle the different situations. There are a few scenarios that can occur which we will look at; the lease expiring, you ending the tenancy, the tenant ending the tenancy and evicting a tenant.

Lease Expiry

It is most common for landlords to let their BTLs for 12 months. Once a lease expires, you have the option to either renew the lease or end the tenancy, each requiring a different course of action.

Chapter 7: Ending the Tenancy

Renewals

Hopefully, you will have no problems with your tenant and will be considering renewing the tenancy. There are two things you can do here, and both processes are straight forward. The first option you have is to simply renew the tenancy. All you will have to do is get a copy of your tenancy agreement and have both of you sign it, dating it from the day the previous agreement ended. You should provide your tenants with the Right to Rent guide if a new version has been released from the time you signed the old tenancy agreement. Also, take advantage of the renewal if you need to change something in the agreement. Perhaps something has not been working well for you. Because this is a new lease agreement, you have the freedom to do some tweaking before signing. Don't do this unnecessarily because this can leave a sour taste in your tenant's mouth, especially with regards to increasing the rent. If you have justifiable reasons to do so, then go for it but hiking up the prices just for the sake of it might cost you a good tenant.

The second option you have is just to let the tenancy roll over. What this means is that you don't sign a new

Chapter 7: Ending the Tenancy

agreement, but the tenant stays on the property and still pays rent without signing a new tenancy agreement. Most terms in your expired AST will still stand. However, it will move to a periodic tenancy under section 5 of The Housing Act 1988, often referred to as "statutory periodic tenancy" because it is created under statute. The payment of rent will define the period of the tenancy. The tenant can stay if they continue to pay in line with the payment schedule specified in the expired AST, and if not, you can ask them to leave. If the rent is paid to you every week, then the tenancy period will be a week to week basis, but usually is monthly. Neither of you are tied down by a fixed-term contract, so it gives you both flexibility to end the tenancy. However, neither of you can just decide to empty the property as notice is required to be given under the Housing Act. The tenant will have to give one month's notice before leaving, and the landlord is still required to give two months' notice. So, there is still protection for both parties in this sense. This type of rolling contract is probably the most convenient because it requires no effort from either party to put in place at the end of a fixed-term tenancy.

There are other options, like issuing a memorandum and drafting a contractual periodic tenancy agreement. The

Chapter 7: Ending the Tenancy

memorandum is just a one-page extension of the previous contract that you can state any changes on, as well as the new signing date and the new date of expiry. The contractual periodic tenancy agreement is similar to letting the tenancy roll over into a statutory periodic tenancy. The key difference here is that there will be a clause in the original tenancy agreement that it will continue after the expiry of the fixed term on a given period (i.e. month to month). Be aware that a contractual periodic tenancy can impact the notice you need to give your tenant when serving a Section 21 notice. You will usually be required to give two months notice, as with a statutory periodic tenancy, unless you are receiving rent payments either quarterly or every six months. In which case you must give three months notice or six months notice. I recommend taking rent weekly or monthly to avoid this situation.

Suppose you have opted to sign a new tenancy agreement. In that case, you must provide the tenant with the "prescribed information", a How to Rent checklist, a Gas Safety Certificate, and an Energy performance certificate. If you are letting the contract roll and turn into a periodic tenancy, then you only need to issue the How to Rent checklist to your tenant if there has been

Chapter 7: Ending the Tenancy

any updates or changes to it. It's worth sending a copy regardless as forgetting to send an updated version of the checklist to your tenant will mean you cannot serve a Section 21 notice when the time comes. Also, make sure that their deposit was protected throughout the tenancy and you can continue on as normal.

Ending the Tenancy

If you want to end the tenancy once the contract is up, you will need to serve a notice on your tenant. There can be multiple reasons why you want to end the agreement. Sometimes, it has nothing to do with the tenant. You might be thinking of selling the property, wanting to renovate it, or just have another tenant lined up — whatever the reason you don't want to continue with the contract.

When requesting to take back possession of the property, you are required to give two months' notice to the tenant before ending the lease. You will not be able to ask the tenant to leave before the end date stipulated in the original tenancy agreement unless there has been a breach in the contract. You should serve the notice in a

Chapter 7: Ending the Tenancy

written format so that you can retain proof of it. This notice is called a Section 21 notice, and it is to be served when the landlord wants to take their property back. You are not required to tell the tenant why you are taking your property back. A Section 21 is not the same as an eviction notice. You will still have to abide by the rules set out in the original tenancy agreement. The same steps apply for ending a periodic or rolling tenancy. Even though there may not be a fixed agreement, you still have to hand out the Section 21 notice and give two months' notice to the tenant.

The tenant may also want to issue you with a surrender notice. This just means that they are the ones that want to leave, so this is their version of a Section 21 notice. They will still have to follow the right steps to do this. The tenant will be able to give you this notice at the end of their current tenancy agreement or during a periodic tenancy. They are required to provide you with one month's notice and are also not required to tell you why they want to leave. Essentially, you cannot do anything to prevent them from leaving. If your tenant does give you this notice, the contract will end and you both can go on your separate ways.

Chapter 7: Ending the Tenancy

Be aware that serving a notice is not ending a tenancy, it is only requesting that the tenancy be ended. Only once both of you have agreed and the tenant leaves and returns the keys to you is the tenancy actually over. If you have a very stubborn tenant, you may need to get a court order to get them to leave. You may also have a tenant who is willing to leave but needs longer than the two months' notice. If it is possible to give them some extra time then do so, especially if they have been good tenants. Regardless of whether you or the tenant has ended the tenancy, if the tenant has met all the requirements stipulated in the tenancy agreement, they are to get the full amount of their deposit back.

Dealing with a Tenant Wanting to Leave Early

In some cases, a tenant will want to leave before the fixed term tenancy has expired. Legally, they will not be able to leave until their contract has expired, unless there is a break clause in your agreement or you both are in mutual agreement. Break clauses allow for the contract to be

Chapter 7: Ending the Tenancy

broken by either party and can be unconditional or can be conditional on specific requirements being met. For example, a break clause may allow either party to break the contract after six months of rent has been fully paid within a 12-month tenancy. However, without a break clause, there is no legal obligation on the tenant or the landlord to enter into negotiating an early ending to the tenancy. Either party can insist on enforcing the contract to its full term. So, your choices are to deny them and enforce the rental payments until the tenancy agreement has expired, or to agree to let them out of the contract.

In my opinion, it is best to negotiate with your tenant and come to an agreement about when they can move out of the property whilst giving you enough time to find a replacement tenant. I always include a break clause into my AST's requiring the tenant to give two months notice should they wish to leave the tenancy early. It is not worth holding the tenant to the contract if they want to go, especially if you think there is a risk they will damage your property.

Terminating a Lease Early

The only reason you should want to terminate a lease early is because your tenant has violated the terms of the lease agreement. Most of the time, this means they have not been paying their rent. This can be extremely infuriating, but also bear in mind the eviction process can be extremely stressful and embarrassing for your tenant and so should always be your last resort to resolving tenancy issues.

The first thing you should do is think about whether eviction is the only way to solve the problem. If the tenant has been fairly good but has recently not been paying their rent or living up to their tenant responsibilities, then perhaps you can work out some sort of deal. Trying to work out a payment plan or just having a conversation about the situation might work for you. The first thing you should do is call your tenant to find out what is going on.

If there is no change, you may find you are only left with the option to terminate the lease. We have already spoken about a Section 21 notice which is issued at the end of a

Chapter 7: Ending the Tenancy

tenancy agreement. The other option is a Section 8 notice, which can be served at any point during the tenancy. The problem with a Section 8 notice is that it does not guarantee the tenant moving out. If they disagree with you, they can remain in the property and you will need to go to court to seek a ruling over your situation. If you are close to the end of the tenancy agreement, it might be best to wait it out and serve the Section 21 notice. Whether you serve a Section 8 or Section 21 notice, the chances of the person moving out are fairly high. Most people will comply with this.

In the case of a really stubborn person that refuses to move out even when given notice, you will have to issue a court order. You must first wait until the notice has expired before going ahead with this. This will give the tenant time to make amends or leave. Now, at the court phase, there is very little you can do. Just make sure you have all proof of correspondence between you and the tenant. Everything you have done up to this point should have written evidence so that nothing can be disputed. You must do everything in your power to prove that you have held up your end of the bargain and have treated the tenant fairly and with respect.

Chapter 7: Ending the Tenancy

If you have won the court case, the tenant should move out. In most cases they will, but unfortunately there are those people that just want to make life harder for themselves and for you. If they do not move out, you cannot go over there and change the locks, or even step onto the property without their knowledge. If you do, you could be charged. Instead, take the proper steps to protect yourself. In this case, you will have to apply for a Warrant of Possession through a County Court Bailiff. You may have to wait a while because a warrant number has to be issued, and even after it has been issued it will go into a queue for a bailiff appointment (The Landlord, 2007a). There are specialised tenant eviction companies that you can consult if you find yourself in this situation and are unsure about how to proceed. They will be able to give you appropriate advice regarding your situation. There will be a fee involved, but in the long run, they might be able to save you money and a lot of effort and frustration.

Chapter 7: Ending the Tenancy

Updates to Section 8 and Section 21

There might be some changes to the Section 21 and Section 8 processes, so be aware of these. The government has announced that they are planning on removing Section 21 of the Housing Act 1988 and improving on Section 8 eviction grounds (Propertymark, n.d.-d). The government is looking to do this to improve the current processes and make them smoother overall. Essentially, they want it to be fairer for both the tenant and the landlord.

An enhanced Section 8 would mean that there would be a quicker system in place for a landlord to evict their current tenant fairly. Essentially, this would result in faster processing through the courts. The tenant will also benefit from the changes because there is expected to be more security for the tenant staying at the property.

Chapter 7: Ending the Tenancy

Checklist and Key Takeaways

- You have two main options when renewing your tenant's lease. You could sign a new tenancy agreement, or you can let the old one roll over on a periodic basis.
- If the tenant wants to end the tenancy early, it is best to come to a mutual agreement and let them out of the lease. This will be less drama for you than trying to get them to stay.
- You can end the tenancy with a Section 21 notice if you are at the end of your tenancy agreement.
- You can end the tenancy in the middle of the tenancy agreement with a Section 8 notice. This can only be done if the tenant has breached the tenancy agreement in some way.
- It is always best to try and resolve any problems with communication and compromise. Eviction should be a last resort because it can take a lot of time and resources.
- If you must evict your tenant, be sure you are following the right processes. Wait until the

Chapter 7: Ending the Tenancy

Section 8 notice has expired before you escalate it to court.

- Make sure you have written proof of all correspondence with the tenant and have followed all the protocols. Anything that you speak about to the tenant must be followed up with a written form of communication.
- If you are confused about something regarding the eviction process, consult a tenant eviction specialist.

Chapter 8: Bookkeeping

Running a BTL is running your own business. As with any other business, you will need to have a plan in place to run your finances. If you don't have a plan in place, then there is a large chance you will mismanage your money and you could end up in a problematic financial situation. If you can set up a sound system earlier on, you will have the time to focus on the other important activities of managing your rental properties and buying new ones.

Setting Up an Effective Bookkeeping System

There are a few steps you can take to make sure you set up an effective bookkeeping system. Your system needs to work well for you and not be complicated. Keeping track of your finances will be the backbone of your BTL business, and so you take the time to set up a system that works for you.

Chapter 8: Bookkeeping

Separate Your Business Accounts from Your Personal Accounts

It can get very confusing for you if all your money is flowing in and out of the same accounts. It will become impossible to tell what goes where, what you can spend, and what needs to be reserved. If you are unable to separate your money, you will not be able to allocate it properly. Having separate accounts may not seem like something you need at the beginning, but it can cause problems for you later on. Not only will having separate accounts help you allocate your money properly, but it will also help you out at tax time by segregating your BTL income from your personal income.

As soon as you start receiving money for your BTL, it is time to open up that business account. All your rental money will go in there, and you will be able to see how much you've got and enable you to plan for your finances. The business account will be where you will hold the money you need for potential vacant periods, repairs, and any other property expenses that may pop up. I like to keep 10% of each months rent for each of my properties to pay for these.

If you have more than one property, I find it helps to have a separate bank account for each one. It becomes complicated having everything together, especially when you are trying to reconcile incoming and outgoings. If you have one account for all your properties, you might not notice that one property is losing money because it will be hidden amongst profits from your other properties. Because each property has to be able to pay for itself, you want to identify and look to resolve any loss-making properties in your portfolio as soon as possible. The separate accounts help to report on each asset and identify the problem ones. Of course, if you have a bad month or two with one property, you can borrow money from other accounts. However, this should only be a temporary thing and you try to keep your properties separate if you want to keep things simple.

Track Your Property Expenses

Having a rental property does come with expenses, just as it comes with income. Not being able to track these expenses means that you don't have visibility on the performance of your asset. You need to be able to track

Chapter 8: Bookkeeping

where your money is coming in from and where it is going out. The mantra "what gets measured gets managed" can be keenly applied to your bookkeeping. When you see what your expenses are, you can gauge what is required and what you can cut back on.

Many landlords use spreadsheets to help them with this. You can easily design your own worksheet to track the flow of your money, but there are also various templates online. Others prefer to use accounting software designed for rental properties. There are a few to choose from, so you can pick the one that works best for you. You can use whatever method works best for you, as long as it effectively tracks what comes in and what goes out.

Tracking your expenses will include anything that you have spent for your property, not just bills. Remember to keep your receipts, because when tax time comes, you will need proof of what you bought for your business. If you have not kept these records, you may not get tax relief, and that is just losing money for no reason.

Chapter 8: Bookkeeping

Choose Between Cash or Accrual Accounting

The cash method and the accrual method are the two main ways you can go about managing your finances. There are pros and cons to both, but both work. The most important thing is that you choose one of them and stick with it.

The cash method is when you don't record income or expenses until they have actually entered or left your account. For example, if your tenant is supposed to pay their rent on the 1st of the month, but they do not pay until a week later on the 8th, you will not recognise the income until you receive it on the 8th. The money has to be physically with you or in your account for you to add it to your books. The same goes for expenses. Even though you know you will be paying the water bill this month, you won't account for it until the money has left your account and the bill has been paid.

The accrual method works by accounting for all transactions when they are made or committed to, rather than when the money is in or out of your account. This way, you will recognise future dated items that you know will be paid to you or taken out of your account. For example, if you take out insurance on the 1st day of the month and you do not have to pay for 30 days, you will recognise the expense on the 1st of the month even though payment will not be made until the 30th. In cash accounting method you will recognise the expense on the 30th of the month when the payment is made from your bank account. The cash method is more straightforward and easier to follow than accrual accounting as you can simply prepare your accounts from your bank statements. If you decide to use an accountant, they will most likely use the accrual method.

Go Digital

Most of the world is already digital, but it is surprising how many people still use paper to store their information. Placing everything in a digital format will allow you to keep track of everything much easier. Less information will get lost, and you will be able to share things easily and conveniently. You can do this by scanning receipts, documents, and invoices onto your computer and then saving it to a cloud-based server so you can access them from anywhere. Popular services are

Dropbox and Google Drive. You can also use digital signing software such as DocuSign or PandaDoc for your tenancy agreements.

Automation

When it comes to dealing with finances, whatever can be automated should be. We often get caught up with other things, and the accounting side of the business can fall to the wayside. Rather than accepting this or letting it happen, automation can make our loads lighter. Instead of having to remember you have to pay for a certain thing every month, setting up automatic payments allows you to not worry about it. Often, delays in payments can mean delays in services. You don't want that, especially if it can be easily avoided. Automate what you can so that you can have more time to do things that are more important.

Chapter 8: Bookkeeping

Be Prepared

A big mistake many people make is trying to solve problems as they come. As much as this sounds like the most logical thing to do, it can cause a huge issue when problems pop up unexpectedly. Always be prepared for future problems, especially if they are going to cost money.

You can use past data to pick up on trends and spikes in spending (another reason why keeping track of your money is so important). For example, if you cover your tenants' utility bills, the electricity bills and maintenance costs will increase in the winter. There are also unexpected things that might happen, like multiple appliances breaking around the same time or maybe you have a longer void period than you thought you would. Will you have the money to replace them if this does happen?

Be Consistent

We often put off things that we do not enjoy doing, and many people do not enjoy reviewing their accounts. Delaying this can cause a major backlog and many other issues when you actually get around to doing it. Since you only have to file for taxes once a year, people only handle their books once a year. Imagine sitting down with all these receipts and invoices at the end of the year, trying to figure out what happened ten months ago. It will be a huge mess, and a headache to deal with.

You should be reviewing your books once a month. If there are any discrepancies, you can deal with them then, since you will be able to recall the situation and what happened. Leaving things for the last minute also opens you up to losing information and making mistakes. Instead, save yourself the trouble of having to sit for days trying to figure out your finances at the end of the year. Spending a few hours at the end of each month is a much better strategy and will make life much easier when figuring out your finances.

Chapter 8: Bookkeeping

Don't Be Afraid to Seek Out a Professional

If you are stuck and have no clue what is going on with this financial thing, consider hiring an accountant. A professional will be able to guide you and show you areas in which you can improve and make your life easier. They will also be able to guide you in choosing the right software or system to help manage your finances. If you do not want to use an accountant forever, consider hiring one until you can get a handle on your finances. Also, always hire someone professional and reputable. If you are going to get a professional to help you, make sure it is someone who has experience in the private rented sector and a good track record.

Taxes

Taxes are something we all love to hate. Unfortunately, it is something we all have to deal with, but if we know what we are doing, it can make the process a lot smoother. Plus, we won't have to pay unnecessary taxes. Nobody wants to pay out more of their income than they

Chapter 8: Bookkeeping

absolutely have to. Business taxes run differently to personal tax, and there are different rules you have to play by. Having a good understanding of this will be beneficial to you throughout your rental business. I have included some considerations on taxes below, however, this is not tax advice and you should seek out advice from a tax professional to clarify what is the best tax structure for you.

The rate of taxes will differ from business to business. It really all depends on what your income was that year and whether you are operating your rental business through a limited company or as an individual. These rates are also subject to change. Make sure you know what tax bracket you fall into that year, as this will help you to plan your taxes for the year.

Due to recent changes to what is allowed as deductible expenditure for individuals in the private rental sector, most landlords now operate through a limited company. This change is for mortgage interest relief, being reduced to 0% for landlords renting properties in their personal name. This means that the mortgage interest will not be allowed as a tax deduction to the rental income from the tax years starting 2020 and after for these landlords. In

Chapter 8: Bookkeeping

contrast, landlords operating through a limited company can still claim a tax deduction for the full mortgage interest amount incurred in the tax year.

Setting up a limited company

As mentioned above, a key advantage for operating your rental business through a limited company is the ability to deduct mortgage interest from the rental income. This is generally one of the larger expense items in a landlord's books and can have a significant impact on your taxable position if not deducted.

Instead of paying individual tax, you will have to pay a corporation tax on your company profits at the end of your company year. The tax rate on company profits is currently 19%, which may work out to be lower than individual tax rates after accounting for personal allowance. This type of tax is on a different time frame than individual income tax as will be aligned to the company tax year, which is determined from the date in which you incorporate the company.

Chapter 8: Bookkeeping

Some considerations for having your BTL portfolio in a limited company are:

- You can get a deduction for mortgage interest, which is not available for individuals anymore.
- You can control the income given to you as an individual so that you can stop payments coming to you if you are about to become a higher rate taxpayer as an individual. This is something you are unable to do if investing in property as an individual because all income flows straight to you.
- There is potential for selling the company that owns the BTL instead of the property itself, which can result in large savings in SDLT.

The difficulties you might have with the limited company include:

- You have to lodge annual accounts to HMRC and companies house.
- You need to maintain more detailed records.
- You will likely need to bring an accountant into your team.
- There is potential that other taxes may be applied on your property, such as taxes on enveloped

Chapter 8: Bookkeeping

> dwellings, which is a tax on properties in a company that each individually have a value more than £500k.

It's important to know about the taxes on taking money out of the company. When the income goes into the company, it belongs to that entity and not an individual. This means when you take cash out of the company, it will form part of your personal income. You can pay yourself from your limited company through dividends or a salary.

Dividends are payments that an individual will receive when they hold a number of shares in a company. It's one way to get cash from the company that's paid to you after the company pays the corporation tax. Once you receive it, you need to pay the taxes on the amount at your personal tax rate.

Another way to take out money through a company is by salary, but you will need to register for PAYE for employers, which means you will have to deduct certain taxes every month. For example, you will need to pay National Insurance to the HMRC.

Chapter 8: Bookkeeping

If you are contemplating using a limited company, you should speak to a tax advisor to make sure it is the best approach for your circumstances. They will also be able to guide you through your reporting obligations and annual compliance costs for the company.

Running your rental business as an individual

For landlords operating their rental business in their personal name and not under a limited company, they will add their taxable rental income to their personal income each year when it comes to reporting their taxes. When you're working out your tax on your rental profit, you have to follow a few steps (Gov.UK, 2017):

1. You will need to calculate your net rental profit. This can be done by taking the total amount you received for the year and subtracting your allowable expenses for the year.
2. Next, deduct your personal allowance for the year. This is the amount you earn before tax.
3. What is left is your taxable income. Depending on which tax bracket you fall under, the amount of tax you pay will vary. Take your total taxable income

Chapter 8: Bookkeeping

and multiply it by the percentage of tax you need to pay.
4. The amount you get will be the tax due on your rental profit.

If you have another job that you are getting an income from, you will have to pay taxes on that figure as well. Make sure that you have proof that you have paid taxes on your other income, otherwise your taxes may be worked out incorrectly. This might result in you paying more than what you need to.

If you have any expenses that were incurred for the sole purpose of your rental business, you may be able to offset these costs against the rental income of your property. For example, if you have bought cleaning materials for your rental property and they are only used to clean your BTL property, you can claim for these. In cases where something has not been bought exclusively for the rental property, you might be able to claim for the portion that is. Claiming for past expenses can only be done in some instances.

You can also claim for maintenance and repair costs for your rental property. This includes typical things such as repairing leaks, electrical faults, broken structures, replacing existing fixtures, and anything that was done to restore (not improve) the property back to its original condition (Gov.UK, 2017).

If you need to replace an old or damaged item in the rental house, this can also be claimed for. However, if the replacement item is an improvement on the old item, you will not be able to claim for more than the value of the old item as if it was bought now. For example, if you needed to buy a replacement for an old sofa in your BTL property, and the equivalent of the old sofa is worth £100, but you bought a new sofa worth £2,000. In that case, you would have improved on the old sofa, and cannot claim for the improvement. Instead, you would have to claim only for the £100, which is the equivalent of the old sofa. You will also be able to claim for the cost of any services needed to dispose of the old sofa or acquire its replacement. If you gained any money from the removal of the old item, for example if you sold the old sofa, you would have to deduct that amount from the total amount you will be claiming for.

If you have more than one property, taxes will not be worked out per property. Rather, the total profit across all your properties must be calculated and given as one

Chapter 8: Bookkeeping

figure. Tax is then calculated from there. If you are running at a loss on one property but have received a profit from the other, your taxable income will be the figure given when you subtract the loss from property one from the profit of property two. If you have made a loss on property one that is more than the profit made from property two, you can claim relief because your property business operated at a loss for that year (year one). These losses will be carried over into the next year (year two), and you will only have to pay tax on the profit of year two after you have subtracted the final loss of year one. In short, if you have made an overall loss, it will be carried forward until your overall profits exceed that amount.

If you decide to let out your property for non-commercial reasons, like letting it out for a friend or family at a reduced rate, you cannot carry over any losses into the next year. For instance, let's say the rent you usually charge for a property is £500 per month, but you let it out to your cousin for £250 per month. The expenses for the property come to £3500 that year, but because you charged less you only got £3000 from your cousin. You ran at a loss of £500 that year, but you will not be able to carry forward that £500 to next year. Instead, it will be taken as though your profit is nil. If you did not charge your cousin at all for the time he lived in the property, you would not be able to claim any expenses for the property.

In the case of joint ownership of a property, tax is worked out per person. First, let's talk about a joint property for a married couple or civil partners. The income and expenses for the property will automatically be split 50:50. If one person owns a higher percentage of the property, then they have to present proof of this by filling out a declaration of beneficial interests in joint property and income (form 17) and notifying HM Revenue and Customs (Gov.UK, 2017). Each person will pay tax on their percentage of the taxable profit.

For any other types of joint properties, each party will pay tax on their agreed percentage of the benefit. This can be owning a property with your friend, parent, business partner, or sibling. The amount of the property each person owns will usually be stipulated when you purchase the property. Your profits and losses will be split according to that agreed-upon percentage.

You can do your own taxes, or you can hire an accountant to do it for you. If you are confused or unsure about something, then it is best to hire a professional to help

Chapter 8: Bookkeeping

you. They will be able to guide you and show you where you can claim tax deductions. Many people opt for getting a professional since it is less work for them, but it is a personal choice. If you do want to hire an accountant, remember to factor that into your budget.

Checklist and Key Takeaways

- Before you even receive your first month's rent, you must set up an effective bookkeeping system.
- When tracking your income and expenses, make sure you account for everything and save all proof.
- Have separate business and personal accounts.
- You should not leave your accounting until the last minute. Be consistent and update your books monthly.
- Keeping everything in a digital format will allow you to keep everything safe and find what you need quickly.
- Choose between a cash or accrual bookkeeping system and stick to it.

Chapter 8: Bookkeeping

- Always have money saved for unexpected scenarios. You never know what might happen, and you need enough liquid money to deal with anything that pops up.
- You will have to file your taxes every year. Make sure you know what tax bracket you fall under.
- Make sure you are careful and accurate when doing your taxes. You do not want to be paying more than you have to.
- If you are unsure about something, hire a professional accountant. They will be able to guide you in the right direction and make sure that both your taxes and general bookkeeping is up to date and accurate.

Chapter 9: Should I Manage It Myself or Hire Someone?

Most of this book has been focused on the self-management of a property, but there may be some cases where it might be wiser to get a letting agent. This is a decision you will have to make for yourself, but it is always best to have all the information before you do so. We will be going through what letting agents are, what they do, what the benefits are of having one, and what options you have when hiring one.

Deciding on Using a Letting Agent

Using a letting agent is not only a money thing. You should look at all the variables and decide if it is the best thing for you to do. There are three key questions or areas that need your attention when making this decision. These areas include the value of your time, deciding what you enjoy, and your confidence to manage your property. Let's dive more into detail with each of these.

Chapter 9: Should I Manage It Myself or Hire Someone?

The first question you should ask yourself is, "What is the value of my time?" If you were to spend a specific amount of time on your property, could that time be used to do something that is more productive, or could ultimately earn you more money? The best way to go about doing this is by putting a monetary value on your time. If you have another job, you can figure out your hourly rate, and that would be the average per hour that your time is worth. If you are running your own business or work for yourself full time, then you can work it out by taking your annual income and dividing it by 1750, the average amount of hours a person works per year. Now, if hiring a letting agent is cheaper than losing the number of hours you would be using to do it yourself, it would be well worth it. If doing it yourself is not going to pull you away from something that could make you more money, then you should consider to manage the property yourself.

The next question you should ask yourself is, "What do I enjoy?" Everyone is different and enjoys different things. Some people really enjoy being a landlord, and it makes them happy to interview potential tenants and rush to the tenant's side when something needs to be repaired. There is genuine joy to be found in being a landlord if that is what you love. On the other hand, other people find it

Chapter 9: Should I Manage It Myself or Hire Someone?

incredibly tedious to go through the interviewing process and have their day interrupted by the needs of a tenant. In this case, they would be dragging their feet every time they have to attend to the tenant. If something needs to be dealt with, the chances are they would not do a very good job of it. These people view the property as an investment, and nothing else. If you are the first person, then you should manage the property yourself. It is something you enjoy, so don't rob yourself of the experience. If you are the second person, then you should consider hiring a letting agent. You will probably end up making yourself and your tenants miserable managing the property poorly.

The final question you should ask yourself to help determine if you should hire a letting agent or not is, "How much confidence do you have in yourself to do the job correctly?" This is probably the most important question since it will ultimately determine whether you will be successful or not. This point will tie back to how much you enjoy being a landlord. If you do, then you will probably have no problem with staying on top of legislation and figuring out better ways to do things. Being a landlord requires skills that vary from knowing the legislation to dealing with people. These skills can

Chapter 9: Should I Manage It Myself or Hire Someone?

grow with time, but you need to be willing to put in the work to foster them. If you are confident that you can do a good job of being a landlord, then go for it. If you are not, then you should consider getting a letting agent to make the process smoother for you.

Another option may be just to get a letting agent for the first year, learn what you need to, and then go off on your own. You can keep an eye on what they are doing and take note of the skills they have. This will leave you in a better position if you are not that confident at the beginning.

All that we have just discussed is just a guideline for you to figure out whether you want to hire a letting agent or not. There may be other factors for you to consider, but it is best that you take the time and weigh up the pros and cons. The cost of the letting agent is not the only thing that you should consider. Rather, look at it holistically, taking into account every factor that will be affected. You should be the one that is confident in your decision.

Chapter 9: Should I Manage It Myself or Hire Someone?

What Does a Letting Agent Do?

A letting agent performs various functions, from finding your tenants to full management of your property. You actually have control over how much you let the agent do. If you just want them to find a tenant for you, you have that option, and then you will do everything else yourself. You can also leave the agent in charge of everything so that you are completely removed from the process. Whatever you choose, just be aware that you will be paying for the services you require. The more you want the letting agent to do, the more you will have to pay.

The prices of various letting agents will also vary from agency to agency and the level of service you are after. I will give a ballpark estimate, but you will have to make enquiries to each letting agent to find out their pricing. For just finding a tenant, you would be looking at a one-off fee that would be around the price of one month's rent at your property. Some agencies have a definitive price, and others will work off the value of your property. If you want the agent to do the rent collection, the fee should be somewhere around 3% of the rent charged to the tenant. Full management of the property can be priced relatively

Chapter 9: Should I Manage It Myself or Hire Someone?

high, so you should budget for between 7% and 15% of the monthly rent, depending on your area. This will allow you to be fully removed from the process. All of these prices are general indications and will differ depending on where the property is situated, the type of property it is, and the letting agency itself.

Some agencies will offer different services than others, so you will have to do some research to find out which ones will suit you best. Some offer more intensive offerings, while others are pretty basic in what they do. It is always a good idea to make sure that you are comfortable with the letting agent you choose. Schedule an interview and ask lots of questions. Essentially, you will be leaving your business in their hands, so you need to be sure you trust them to handle it properly.

Let's go through each of the most common responsibilities in a bit more detail, so that you can fully understand what you will be paying for. The most basic service that a letting agent provides is being responsible for finding a suitable tenant for you, and handling the whole process until the tenant has signed the tenancy agreement. They will go to your property, take photos and advertise your property on various platforms. Once they

Chapter 9: Should I Manage It Myself or Hire Someone?

have gotten a few interested parties, they will go through the tenant screening process. You can choose to be involved here or not. The letting agent will arrange the property viewings and attend them on your behalf. Once they have found a suitable tenant, they will make sure that all the proper documentation has been signed by both the tenant and you. They will also perform all the necessary checks on the tenant. Once the tenant has signed the agreement and has moved in, the letting agent's job is done and you are now in charge going forward.

For the rent collection option, some agencies offer this with the finding of a tenant. The agent will act as the middleman for the transfer of money between the tenant and you. They will collect the deposit and protect it and collect the rent from the tenant. If the tenant is not paying their rent on time, it is the agent's responsibility to chase after the tenant until they do. It will also be their responsibility to issue notices if it is necessary. You will also be able to rely on the letting agent to inform you and give you advice on what to do next and how to handle situations where the tenant is not paying rent.

Chapter 9: Should I Manage It Myself or Hire Someone?

The full managing option is where the letting agent will take on almost all the tasks that the landlord would be responsible for. This includes finding a tenant and collecting the rent. Other services that are included here are doing property inspections, inventory checks, corresponding with the tenant, organising any maintenance that has to be done on the property, and handling any disputes.

It is important to note that whether or not you choose to hire a letting agent, the responsibility and liability of the property is yours. Since the property is under your name and belongs to you, if anything happens it is still your responsibility. You can be removed from the nitty-gritty of the process, but it is still a good idea to be aware of what is going on with your property.

The service you choose to use will all depend on how involved you want to be. Some people want to take on the full landlord function but need a little help, whereas others would rather just be investors and have someone else take care of the rest. Ask yourself why you want to get into property management and then think through which option will be best suited for you. You can also go to letting agents for advice. They do offer this service if

Chapter 9: Should I Manage It Myself or Hire Someone?

you just need some direction and nothing else. Always use a reputable letting agent, and do some research on the internet to see what others have to say about them. It would be even better if you knew someone who used their services before because then you can get firsthand information.

Picking the Right Agent

There are plenty of letting agents out there, and you need to be sure that you are picking the one that is right for you. Research does play a big part in this, but there will come a time when you will have to interview them. This is where you will get a feel for whether this person is going to be the right fit. Remember, this person is going to be representing you to your tenants. You want someone who you are comfortable with and who you are confident can do their job well.

Take some time to sit down with your prospective letting agent and ask them as many questions as you can. Pay attention to their answers and don't be afraid to share any concerns with them. They should be able to answer you clearly and give you advice on how to deal with the

Chapter 9: Should I Manage It Myself or Hire Someone?

concerns you have. You should ask them what kind of tenants they are planning on placing in your property. At this point you should have already discussed your property, so they should have some context surrounding it. Finding the right tenants is one of the most important parts of their job, so you want to make sure that they are able to do this properly. If they are planning to place a family in a small apartment that is better suited for singles and students, take that as a red flag. They have either not listened to you when you were explaining your property or just aren't that experienced.

You should also find out how long it usually takes for them to place a tenant. You can gauge as to whether the agent is good at their job by the length of time they need to fill a property. If the time it takes them is longer than expected, this is an indication that they are not effective at placing tenants. You should also be wary if they give a very short time frame. This could indicate that they are lying, or that they just pick the first person that shows interest. Speak to multiple agents to notice any outliers here.

Another important thing to find out from the letting agent is how they would handle a tenant if they have

Chapter 9: Should I Manage It Myself or Hire Someone?

fallen into arrears. The agent should already have these plans in place and should be able to give you a concrete answer regarding this. They should be well versed in all the legal requirements and have a good understanding of the required paperwork.

The agent will need to visit the property, carry out inspections, and make sure that everything is running smoothly. You should find out how often they plan on visiting the property and giving you feedback. You want someone who will keep you in the loop and who is going to make a point of taking care of the property. Essentially, you should be able to call the agent up at any time to find out how your property is doing, and they should be able to give you an update.

The types of questions you should ask the agent will differ depending on what you want them to do for you. If you are planning on letting them fully manage your property, then you should ask them to explain how they would handle difficult tenants and other important scenarios. If you just want them to find your tenants, then you can keep your questions specific to their tenant searching, screening and placing process.

Chapter 9: Should I Manage It Myself or Hire Someone?

It is a legal requirement for every letting agent to be part of a redress scheme and a Client Money Protection (CMP) scheme. Make sure to enquire about this. If they are not, they are breaking the law and you should not do any business with them. You should also make sure they are registered with the Property Ombudsmen and are a member of a professional organisation. Such as memberships to the Royal Institute of Chartered Surveyors (RICS), the National Approved Letting Scheme (NALS), or the Association of Residential Letting Agents (ARLA).

Online Agents

We live in a world where everything is moving online (if it hasn't already). Letting agents are no exception. You can get really great service from online letting agents for a fraction of the price. Their main function is to find you a suitable tenant, and they can do that at a marginally lower price than the traditional letting agents. You won't be able to meet them face to face, but that shouldn't be a problem. Most of them are very responsive to email and phone calls.

Chapter 9: Should I Manage It Myself or Hire Someone?

To get started with an online letting agency, all you have to do is go to their website and follow the steps. You will then have to pay a fee and upload the details of your rental property. Once you have done this, your property will be distributed across various online property portals. From here, all you have to do is wait for an interested potential tenant. Any interested parties would have to click on your property and make an enquiry, which are sent straight to you. You can then go through them and schedule viewings with the ones you like. This is usually the end of the services offered by an online letting agency, although there are some that offer managed services as well.

In a nutshell, you will be paying a small fee and getting your property advertised on all online platforms, as well as gaining access to all the documents and templates you need for signing a tenancy, email and telephone support, and a tenant referencing service. This is what usually comes with the tenant finding option. For a more comprehensive service, you will have to take out a fully-managed service option. The fee here will be higher, but still much cheaper than your traditional letting agent. Most of their contracts are also offered month to month, so you can opt-out at any point. An online letting agent

Chapter 9: Should I Manage It Myself or Hire Someone?

also has to be part of a redress scheme. If they are not, that means they are operating illegally. If you are operating on a budget, then an online letting agent could be the way to go.

Property Management Software

Property management software is designed to make your life as a landlord easier. It will help you keep everything related to managing your property in one place. There are multiple to choose from, and each of them varies slightly in what they offer. In general, a landlord would use this software to store data, set reminders, and track expenses and income. It is not a requirement to use property management software, but it helps when you are managing many properties. If this is you or if you are planning on growing your portfolio, then it is a good idea to see what is on offer.

There are both free and paid options when it comes to this software. If you really want just the absolute basics, then you can go for the free versions, but the truth is that you will get what you pay for. So, if you are not paying

Chapter 9: Should I Manage It Myself or Hire Someone?

anything, you shouldn't expect too much. Paid software will offer a lot more and it will be easier to navigate and interact with.

If you want to, you can probably keep track of the important things using a spreadsheet. They are the starting point and the go-to solution for most landlords. Eventually, you will get to a point where you want something a bit more sophisticated than a spreadsheet, or you may not feel confident using excel. If this is you, then it will be worthwhile investigating some software solutions. They often a different range of services depending on the package which may include; forecasting, allow you to work out your annual rental income tax using HMRC guidelines, create financial reports, and create and access tenant and maintenance management reports. If you are interested in a good property management software, some that I am aware of are:

- Landlord Vision (paid)
- Property Portfolio Software (paid)
- PropertyHawk (free)
- Smart Property Manager (free)

Chapter 9: Should I Manage It Myself or Hire Someone?

Checklist and Key Takeaways

- In some cases, using a letting agent is the best option. You should decide whether you want to be a landlord and take on all of those duties, or if you just want to be an investor and have someone else manage the property.
- There are various functions a letting agent can perform. It is up to you how much or how little you want them to do.
- Understand each function and how much they will be doing. You should know how involved you want to be.
- When choosing a letting agent, make sure you spend time asking the right questions. You are choosing someone to represent you and your business, so don't take that lightly.
- Make sure that the letting agent you choose is part of a redress scheme and has the necessary experience.
- Online agents are a great option if you want to have a letting agent, but are on a budget.

Chapter 9: Should I Manage It Myself or Hire Someone?

- Property management software can help you keep track of all the necessary information when dealing with your BTL. You should consider it if you want something more than just a way to track expenses.

Conclusion

There is a lot of information and skills required to run a successful BTL. It is not simply buying a property and finding someone to live in it. You must be able to handle your finances and taxes properly, understand how to deal with your tenants, be well versed in the legal requirements, and the list goes on.

It can be argued that the most important thing about running a BTL is the property. It is what you are offering, and it is the thing that will make you money. Don't treat this lightly; you must do your best to take care of your property. When you rent out your house you want someone else to look after it, so if you expect this of someone else, you must first set the example. Don't just do things for the sake of it or try and find the cheapest way out. Not giving your BTL the attention it needs will come back to bite you in the future. There is nothing worse than everything breaking and falling apart at the same time. The type of property you present to the world will dictate the type of tenant you attract. If you want someone who will take pride in where they live and do

Conclusion

their best to care for the property, the property itself must reflect that.

Besides the property itself, the most important thing is your tenants. They are what could let you have a great and easy experience, or could make your life miserable. That is why it is so essential to start in the right place. You need to know the type of tenant you want to have before you even start looking for them. Take a look at your property and decide what kind of person would fit in perfectly, then market accordingly. When you begin viewings and interviews, you should also have your eyes open for any red flags. Remember not just to meet and greet your potential tenants, but also look at other subtle things. You will know when there is something off, so trust your gut. If you are lucky enough to find a perfect tenant, keep them happy and hold on to them for as long as you can.

If you take care of your property and get the right tenants, you will have the hardest part sorted. If you decide that you do not want to be involved in all of that tenant searching and property management, then you don't have to be. You can hire a property manager to do that work for you. It is all a matter of preference and

Conclusion

deciding what is going to suit you and your lifestyle the best.

Now that you have completed the book, I would suggest you go back and try and implement some of the things that I have spoken about. If you do not have a bookkeeping system set up, then it is about time you start implementing one. If you have not considered whether you should hire a property manager or not, then write out a list of pros and cons and identify what would be best for you. If you have not considered how you will be marketing your BTL, see what you have to offer and find ways to reach your target tenant. If there has been something that really stuck out to you in this book, I challenge you to do something with the information. Implement it in some way, or develop a new plan. The best way to learn and get good at something is through practical application and consistency.

You now have all the basic knowledge you need to run your BTL successfully. This builds a strong foundation for you to build your property business. If done right, you will reap the rewards of high returns and a stable passive income. You will also be able to avoid the common pitfalls of misunderstanding legislation, not being aware

Conclusion

of your duties as a landlord, mismanaging tenants, and not selecting the right tenants to move into your property. Remember always to be willing to learn. In this business things can change quite quickly, so make sure you are always keeping up to date with the latest rules and regulations.

As you go through your BTL journey, you will gain more experience and more confidence. Maybe you will want to add more properties to your portfolio or decide that you are satisfied with what you have. Whatever your property journey looks like, I hope you find this book has provided you with a strong foundation to help you successfully manage your BTL.

Did you like this book? Leave a review

As an independent author with a small marketing budget, reviews are my livelihood on this platform. If you enjoyed this book, I would really appreciate it if you took just 60 seconds to leave your honest feedback. You can do so by clicking the link below or scanning the below QR code. I love hearing from my readers and I personally read every single review.

>>Click here to leave a 60 second review<<

Or point your camera here to do the same:

References

Basingstoke and Deane. (n.d.). *Housing health and safety rating system*. Basingstoke and Deane. https://www.basingstoke.gov.uk/safety-rating-system

Collatz, A. (2017, January 6). *7 Renter Screening Warning Signs That Aren't So Obvious*. SmartMove. https://www.mysmartmove.com/SmartMove/blog/7-tenant-screening-warning-signs-not-obvious.page

Entwistle, T. (2014, August 13). *Checking Tenants In and Out*. LandlordZONE. https://www.landlordzone.co.uk/information/checking-tenants-in-and-out/

Esajian, P. (n.d.). *Rental Property Accounting & Bookkeeping Tips*. FortuneBuilders. https://www.fortunebuilders.com/rental-property-accounting/

GoCardless. (n.d.). *Landlords: Should you be using Direct Debit?* Gocardless.Com.

https://gocardless.com/guides/posts/how-landlords-use-dd/

Gov.UK. (n.d.-a). *Check your tenant's right to rent.* GOV.UK. https://www.gov.uk/check-tenant-right-to-rent-documents

Gov.UK. (2017, April 6). *Examples of how to work out Income Tax when you rent out a house.* GOV.UK. https://www.gov.uk/guidance/income-tax-when-you-rent-out-a-property-case-studies

Gov.UK. (n.d.-b). *Renting out your property (England and Wales).* GOV.UK. https://www.gov.uk/renting-out-a-property/making-repairs

Gov.UK. (n.d.-c). *Tenancy agreements: a guide for landlords (England and Wales).* GOV.UK. https://www.gov.uk/tenancy-agreements-a-guide-for-landlords/tenancy-types

Hall, Z. D. (2018, February 12). *Looking for the perfect buy-to-let tenant? The Telegraph.* https://www.telegraph.co.uk/property/landlord-guide/find-the-perfect-tenant/

Housing Hand. (n.d.). *What is a guarantor? Housing Hand - The Award-Winning Rent Guarantor.* Housing Hand. https://www.housinghand.co.uk/news/what-is-a-guarantor/

Ikavalko, K. (2018, November 10). *A Landlord's Guide to Renting Furnished or Unfurnished Properties- Liv Rent Blog.* Liv Rent Blog. https://liv.rent/blog/2018/11/furnished-vs-unfurnished-rental-guide-for-landlords/

Ministry of Housing, Communities and Local Government. (n.d.). *A New Deal for Renting: A Consultation - Frequently Asked Questions.* https://assets.publishing.service.gov.uk/government/uploads/system/uploads/attachment_data/file/819738/A_New_Deal_for_Renting_-_Frequently_Asked_Questions_for_Landlords_and_Tenants.pdf

Ministry of Housing, Communities and Local Government. (2006, May 26). *Housing health and safety rating system (HHSRS): guidance for landlords and property-related professionals.* GOV.UK.

https://www.gov.uk/government/publications/housing-health-and-safety-rating-system-guidance-for-landlords-and-property-related-professionals

Ministry of Housing, Communities and Local Government. (2019a). *Landlord and tenant rights and responsibilities in the private rented sector.* https://www.cheshirewestandchester.gov.uk/documents/housing/private-rented-sector/landlord-and-tenant-rights-and-responsibilities-in-the-private-rented-sector-031019.pdf

Ministry of Housing, Communities and Local Government. (2019b, May 31). *How to let.* GOV.UK. https://www.gov.uk/government/publications/how-to-let/how-to-let

Not Letting Go. (n.d.). *How to Be a Good Landlord. No Letting Go Inventory Management.* https://nolettinggo.co.uk/blog/how-to-be-a-good-landlord/

NRLA. (n.d.-a). *A Simple Guide For Landlords | Landlord Guides. Residential Landlords Association.*

https://www.rla.org.uk/landlord/guides/simple-guide-to-being-a-landlord.shtml

NRLA. (n.d.-b). *Top Tips For Landlords | Landlord Guides | RLA*. Www.Rla.Org.Uk. https://www.rla.org.uk/landlord/guides/top-tips-for-landlords.shtml

Prime Location. (2019, January 22). *Should you let your property furnished or unfurnished? | PrimeLocation*. Prime Location. https://www.primelocation.com/discover/landlords-developers-and-investors/furnished-or-unfurnished/

Property Geek. (2017, December 26). *Should you self-manage or use a letting agent?* Property Geek. https://www.propertygeek.net/article/self-manage-or-letting-agent/

Property Vista. (2017, October 26). *Rental Property Accounting: 9 Tips to Keep Your Finances in Order (and the Tax Man Happy)*. Www.Leapdfw.Com. https://www.leapdfw.com/blog/rental-property-accounting-tips/

Property24. (2016, August 25). *Pros and Cons Of Letting Unfurnished Vs Furnished Property - Property24*. Www.Property24.Com. https://www.property24.com/articles/pros-and-cons-of-letting-unfurnished-vs-furnished-property/24563

Propertymark. (n.d.-a). *Tenant Evictions: The Do's and Don'ts. Propertymark.* Retrieved July 3, 2020, from https://www.propertymark.co.uk/advice-and-guides/landlords/eviction-do-s-and-don-ts/

Propertymark. (n.d.-b). *What Does a Letting Agent Do? - Propertymark.* Www.Propertymark.Co.Uk. https://www.propertymark.co.uk/advice-and-guides/landlords/what-does-a-letting-agent-do/

Propertymark. (n.d.-c). *What is tenant referencing?* Propertymark. https://www.propertymark.co.uk/advice-and-guides/landlords/tenant-referencing/

Propertymark. (n.d.-d). *What to do if your tenant hasn't paid rent.* Propertymark. https://www.propertymark.co.uk/advice-and-guides/landlords/rent-arrears/

Propertymark. (n.d.-e). *What's Happening to Section 8 and Section 21?* Propertymark. Retrieved July 3, 2020, from https://www.propertymark.co.uk/advice-and-guides/landlords/whats-happening-to-section-8-and-section-21/

The Landlord. (n.d.-a). *Assured Shorthold Tenancy Agreements Info, Guides & Downloads.* Property Investment Project. https://www.propertyinvestmentproject.co.uk/blog/assured-shorthold-tenancy-agreement/

The Landlord. (n.d.-b). *Everything Landlords Need To Know About Finding Good Tenants.* Property Investment Project. https://www.propertyinvestmentproject.co.uk/blog/finding-tenant-guides-for-landlords/

The Landlord. (2007a). *How Landlords Can Evict Tenants - Getting rid of bad tenants.* Property Investment Project. https://www.propertyinvestmentproject.co.uk/blog/how-to-evict-tenants/

The Landlord. (2007b). *Tips On How To Be A Good Landlord To Your Tenant.* Property Investment

Project. https://www.propertyinvestmentproject.co.uk/blog/be-good-to-your-tenant/

The Landlord. (2008). *Landlord Inventory Guide & Template Form.* Property Investment Project. https://www.propertyinvestmentproject.co.uk/blog/property-inventory-form/

The Landlord. (2010). *How Landlords Can Avoid Bad Tenants.* Property Investment Project. https://www.propertyinvestmentproject.co.uk/blog/avoiding-professional-bad-tenants/

The Landlord. (2011). *Tenancy Application Form.* Property Investment Project. https://www.propertyinvestmentproject.co.uk/blog/tenancy-application-form/

The Landlord. (2012). *How Much Rent Should I Charge My Tenants?* Property Investment Project. https://www.propertyinvestmentproject.co.uk/blog/how-much-rent-should-i-charge/

The Landlord. (2013). *Early Signs Of Potentially Awful Tenants.* Property Investment Project. https://www.propertyinvestmentproject.co.uk/blog/the-early-signs-of-potentially-awful-tenants/

The Landlord. (2014a). *How To End / Terminate A Tenancy Agreement With A Tenant.* Property Investment Project. https://www.propertyinvestmentproject.co.uk/blog/end-terminate-tenancy-agreement/

The Landlord. (2014b). *How To Renew A Tenancy Agreement With a Tenant.* Property Investment Project. https://www.propertyinvestmentproject.co.uk/blog/renew-tenancy-agreement/

The Landlord. (2020a). *List Of The Best Landlord Associations 2020.* Property Investment Project. https://www.propertyinvestmentproject.co.uk/blog/which-is-the-best-landlords-association-which-should-i-join/

The Landlord. (2020b). *List Of The Best Online Letting Agents in 2020.* Property Investment Project. https://www.propertyinvestmentproject.co.uk/blog/online-letting-agents/

The Landlord. (2020c). *Tenant Security Deposit & Protection [Landlord Guide 2020].* Property Investment Project.

https://www.propertyinvestmentproject.co.uk/blog/tenancy-deposit-protection-easy-guide/

The Landlord. (2020d). *Which Landlord Property Management Software Is The Best in 2020?* Property Investment Project. https://www.propertyinvestmentproject.co.uk/blog/which-landlord-software-do-you-recommend-and-which-is-the-best/

Thomas, H. (2015, June 2). *How to be a good landlord - without being taken for a ride.* This Is Money. https://www.thisismoney.co.uk/money/guides/article-3106649/How-good-landlord-without-taken-ride.html

Thompson, S. (n.d.). *Five bookkeeping mistakes by landlords.* Landlord Money Saving. http://landlordmoneysaving.com/five-bookkeeping-mistakes-by-landlords/

Printed in Great Britain
by Amazon